POVERTY POINT
LEGENDS & LORE

POVERTY POINT
LEGENDS & LORE

Jon L. Gibson

THE
History
PRESS

Published by The History Press
Charleston, SC
www.historypress.com

Copyright © 2021 by Jon L. Gibson
All rights reserved

First published 2021

Manufactured in the United States

ISBN 9781467149839

Library of Congress Control Number: 2021938399

In memory of Mitchell Hillman, the fox-man.

He came in the night. The tracks encircled our string-outlined excavation units, almost as if he had peered down at the old construction dirt beneath his feet. At the unit we called the "Five-Legged Spider" Pit because of the mutant or injured arachnid that spun its daily web therein, he hunkered down and hung his head over the edge. What did he see? What did he know?

—Shilombish and the Crystal Drill

CONTENTS

CONTENTS

PREFACE

Poverty Point takes its name from an antebellum "back-country" plantation that once occupied its grounds, a name born of a humorous game of "poor-mouthing" among neighboring planters, whose own plantations were called Hard Times and Hard Bargain.

Several weeks each summer saw the return of tribalism and egalitarian society to Poverty Point. Several weeks each summer saw hard labor conducted without the need for bosses or grievance committees. Several weeks each summer saw young people commune with the living spirit of ancient hallowed grounds. Several weeks each summer saw bonds of friendship form that remain until this day.

Many of the stories told here come out of this shared experience. Folklore, they have become, but they were real experiences once upon a time, when, for a few weeks each summer, the world was a magical place.

I consider myself privileged to have been part of it.

Jon L. Gibson
Lake Claiborne, Louisiana
summer solstice, 2020

ACKNOWLEDGEMENTS

Anything I write about Poverty Point bears the indelible imprint of James Ford for inspiration, Clarence Webb for guidance, Mitchell Hillman for insight and Carl Alexander for generosity. My time spent at Poverty Point is gilded by Mitchell and Ann Hillman and Dennis and Janice LaBatt with friendship; Irvin Arledge, Mark Fox, David Griffing, Stanley Morgan and Orvis Scott with information sharing; Mary Borden, Nancy Clendenen, Bonnie Jean and Timmy Hale, Christine Linson, Levon Morrow, Robert Pickering, Lisa Simpkins, George Skipper and Blondel Surles with down-home conviviality; and Geraldine Coleman, Belinda Corley, Ann Hillman, Wendy Hillman, Gloria Lemon and Betty Miller with country cooking (suppers). Sponsors over the years have included: Sue Bridges, Clarence Webb, J.E. Chance & Associates Inc., Louisiana Division of Archaeology and Louisiana Office of State Parks, and in-kind support came from my home base, the University of Southwestern Louisiana (now, the University of Louisiana, Lafayette, or ULL).

I am grateful to many fine folks for special help at the podium, in the field and in the field and university labs: (lectures) Thurman Allen, John Belmont, Sam Brookes, Lee Buras, John "Houn" Calhoun, Bob Connolly, Joan Exnicios, Glen Greene, David Griffing, Bill Haag, Chris Hays, Ed Jackson, Marvin "Dr. J" Jeter, Jay "Dr. Jay" Johnson, Carl Kuttruff, Jenna Kuttruff, Dennis LaBatt, Burney McClurkan, Bob Neuman, Roger Saucier, Joe Saunders, Tom Sever, Parris Stripling, George Stuart, Donna Thomas, Arville Touchet, Clarence Webb, Rich Weinstein, Steve Williams and

Debbie Woodiel; (fieldwork) John Calhoun, Wade Carr, Lisa Coleman, Sylvia Duay, Janet Delgahausen, James "Fogie" Fogleman, Glen Greene, Mitchell Hillman, Billie Hudson, Ed Jackson, Daniel Jeter, Marvin Jeter, Drew Johnson, Jay Johnson, Carl Kuttruff, Jack Marwitt, Fred Mayer, Burney McClurkan, Sean MuCulley, "Chip" McGimsey, Tom McIntyre, Stanley Morgan, Allen Pesnell, Dawn (McCulley) Pesnell, Terri Prickett, Joe Saunders, Lynn Shreve, Arville Touchet, Greg Vaughan, Rich Weinstein and Dan Whatley; (field lab and university lab work) Linda Alyea, Sandy Ashy, Rosalin Augustine, Danielle Bacque, Jeanne Baker, Erica Bammel, Pam Benoit, Carline Berard, Kathleen "K.B." Bergeron, Rachelle Billeaud, Karon Boudreaux, Julie Bridges, Sue Bridges, Angelo Brigola, Gretchen Broussard, David Buys, Zawn Burdick, Edith Carey, Lisa Coleman, Bob Connolly, Ashleigh D'Aunoy, Eve Dawkins, Leslie Delaney, Charlotte Donald, Debra Ellis, Johnnie Emory, Patricia Farru, Aimee Finley, Linda Fuqua, David Genest, Candance Gossen-Istre, Ruby Hamilton, Kerry Hart, June Hayes, Barry Hillman, Sara Hoffpauir, Thomas Hotard, Michelle Hutchins, Ellen Ibert, Gregory Klingman, Vickie Kountz, Kevin Marks, Thomas Markese, Fred Mayer, Dawn McCulley, Mark Melancon, Patrice Myer, Chad Nunez, Linda Peters, Cathy Pomier, Christine Quebedeaux, Kathleen Sauser, Donna Savoie, Lynn Shreve, Brock Sickey, Christy Simon, Sharon Simoneaux, Annette Sonnier, Agnes Venable, Darrell Venable and Walter Welch; (special services/studies) Thurman Allen, Paul Baker, Richard Birdseye, Carroll Butts, Brian Catlin, Bob Connolly, James Doolittle, James Feathers, Rob Floyd, John Fortner, Douglas Frink, Mary Beth Gibson, Doug Gillette, Glen Greene, Dan Lee, Rolfe Mandel, Fred Mayer, Frank Miller, Billy Moore, Wilber Peak, Mike Russo, Tom Sever, Jerry Shows, Arville Touchet and Sam Valastro.

Most of all, I am indebted to the scores of field school students and volunteers who traveled this memorable path with me over the years. Most of these stories occurred on their watch. Much obliged:

1983: Edith Carey, Janet Delgahaussen, Sylvia Duay, J.R. Fix, Mike Gary, Melissa Green, Donna Gwin, John Guy, Paul Harder, Orland Kalente, Mike Konvika, Dawn McCulley, Bobby Meza, Louis Niva, Terri Prickett, Mark Steilper, Gilbert Wilcox, Larry Wilcox and Tracey Windham.

1985: Dawn Andrews, Michael Antenucci, Jeff Baker, Steve Batug, Madeline Bienek, Mary Bordelon, Alan Bostwick, John Calhoun, Wade Carr, Christy Childers, Leslie Cook, Jan Delgahaussen, Sylvia Duay, Mark Gilbeau, Jeffery

Guillory, Donna Guin, Art Holman, Jeffery Hudson, Lisa Maroon, James Mather Jr., Dawn McCulley, Tom McIntyre, Becky Owens, Terri Prickett, Gina Russell, Kathleen Sauser, Evelyn Sawvel, Nancy Starr, Judy Storey, James Underwood, William Wilkerson, Ooh Foong Yap and Cindy Ziewitz.

1988: Tina Aguiar, Aaron Alexander, Cathy Alyea, Jeanne Baker, Paul Baker, Bryan Bell, Karon Boudreaux, John Calhoun, Julie Castille, Catherine Carmena, Lisa Coleman, Eve Dawkins, Janet Delgahausen, Sylvia Duay, Lena Dupuis, Barb Fisher, Michelle Haj, June Hayes, Connie Heugle, Thomas Hotard, Daniel Jeter, Drew Johnson, Ted Johnson, Slavke Jovanovic, Thomas Markese, Fred Mayer, John Mayer, Shawn McCulley, Barbara Meek, Stan Morgan, Allen Pesnell, Dawn (McCulley) Pesnell, Terri Prickett, Frank Riggle, Rita Rivere, Brett Russell, Jeff Schmitt, Andy Shaw, Greg Vaughan, Dan Whatley, Ed Viguerie and Cindy Ziegler.

1989: Kathy Alyea, Paul Baker, Nicole Blair, John Bonin, Karon Boudreaux, Kim Broussard, Carl Brown, Yvonne Caire, John Calhoun, Lisa Coleman, Kempton Collins, Marc D'Annoy, Albert Davis, Janet Delgahausen, Rebecca Delgahausen, Charlotte Donald, Raymond Dore, Sylvia Duay, Johnny Duplantis, Rita Foreman, Brooks Friedburg, Erin Gibson, Ernie Hilgeman, Richard Hilgeman, Billie Hudson, Dan Jeter, Justin Justice, Ty Landry, Darla Maida, Fred Mayer, Shawn McCulley, Ron McDermitt, Allen Pesnell, Dawn (McCulley) Pesnell, Lane Prejean, Genie Saab, Elizabeth Suire, Charles "Tribbey" Thornton, Susan Thornton, Ryland Witten-Smith and Greg Vaughan.

1991: Erica Bammel, Margaret Barre, Carline Berard, Kathleen Bergeron, Tommy Bourque, Chad Breaux, Mary Buller, Lisa Coleman, Denise Decuir, Natalie "Gnat" DesOrmeaux, Aimee Finley, Jimmy "Fogie" Fogleman, Andree Fortier, June Hayes, Barry Hillman, Billie Hudson, Shannon Hughes, Michelle Hutchins, David Kent, Vickie Kountz, Sonya LaComb, Fred Mayer, John Mayer, Patrice Myer, Chad "E-Rat" Nunez, Doug Palombo, Mike Pears, Helen Perilloux, Angel Quin, Donna Savoie, Lynn Shreve, Sharon Simoneaux, Donna Trahan, Darrel Venable and David Vige.

1993: Linda Alyea, Sandy Ashy, Danielle Bacque, Pam Benoit, Kathleen Bergeron, Shannon Bernard, Rachelle Billeaud, Donny Bourgeois, Angelo Brigolo, Gretchen Broussard, Zawn Burdick, David Buys, John Calhoun, John Clune, Ashleigh D'Aunoy, Gail DeHart, Leslie Delaney, Tim Delaney,

Debra Ellis, Johnnie Emory, Sean Ezell, Patricia Farru, Brit Fontenot, Linda Fuqua, David Genest, James Gist, Ruby Hamilton, Kerry Hart, Sara Hoffpauir, Ellen Ibert, Frank Kincel, Gregory Klingman, Carl Kuttruff, Forest Lemoine, Thomas Marckese, Kevin Marks, Mark Melancon, Alan Morgan, Linda Peters, Cathy Pomier, Bryan Potier, Christine Quebedeaux, Lynn Shreve, Christy Simon, Sharon Simoneaux, Annette Sonnier, Agnes Venable, Darrel Venable, Walter Welch, Alyssa Williams, Jena Wilson and Troy Wingerter.

1995: Sandra Ashy, Danielle Bacque, Kathleen Bergeron, Rachelle Billeaud, Tara Borque, Angelo Brigola, Yvonne Caire. RoAnna Carriere, Katherine Croft, Leslie Delaney, Kay Doré, Debra Ellis, Johnnie Emory, Nicole "Carrots" Everett, Patricia Furru, Gregory Gaspard, Ruby Hamilton, Ted Hampton, Kerry Hart, Shelly "Peas" Hermis, Sara Hoffpauir, Kelly Kimball, Greg Klingman, Coryne LaBry, Elizabeth Landry, Mark Melancon, Cinthia Minnaert, Charles Parker, Ellen Ibert-Parker, Catherine Pomier, Azar Rejaie, Michael Richard, Mary Smith, Greg Vaughan and Walter Welch.

1998: Allen Benjamin, Kathleen Bergeron, Carl Brasseaux, Ryan Brasseaux, Steven Caricutt, Louis Courville, Chris Cring, Gail Dehart, Leslie Delaney, Robin Faulk, Christopher Gray, Christy Hardy, James Hebert, Kirsten Pourroy Hebert, Leslie Hebert, Hans Heinen, Mark Hempen, Kim Jester, Tommy Johnson, Tracey Jones, Miranda LaBatt, Jill Laufer, Nicole de Launay, Tina Loe, Mike McMilleon, Mike Nassiri, Jim Palmintier, Shane Poche, Sanjay Raghavan, Jennifer Ritter, Cherie Royer, Manju Sadarangani, Breanne Sargent, Robert Saunders, Duane Scott, Alison Sims, Mary Sisley, Josette van der Koogh and Robin Watkins.

The illustration on page 44 reproduces figure 40 in Gibson, *Archaic Earthworks*. The original figure was digitally remastered by Diana Greenlee from a figure I drew using data provided by Robert Patten. The University of Louisiana, Monroe, permitted its use. Carl Alexander gave me the comet photograph on page 49; Danielle Bacque, the photographs on pages 23 (*right*), 25, 57 and 61; and James Doolittle, the radar image on page 91 (*below*). Lisa Coleman contributed the field photographs on page 53. Shelia Lewis furnished the aerial photographs (page 91, *left*). Dawn McCulley donated the photograph of the fallen tree on page 48. Tom Sever made available the TMS photograph on page 93. Donna Trahan drew the figures on pages 23 (*below*), 68, 70 and 74. I drew the others on pages 27, 32–34, 36, 37 (*right*), 38 (*above and left*), 39–41, 43 (*opposite and right*), 46, 50, 64–65, 73, 75, 82, 85, 97, 99, 103 and 105 and also took the photograph on page 39 (*above*). The cover illustrations are also by my hand.

Thanks, Dennis, for helping send the message in a bottle to the guardians and for relating several of the following stories. Thanks, Mary Beth, for encouraging me to tell these stories again and for seeing to the compilation's initial critical reads. Thanks, Erin, for translating cyber-speak when I needed.

Thanks to Joe Gartrell for managing this project with panache and to Ashley Hill for polishing the prose, grammar and style. Cameron Thomas designed the cover.

ONCE UPON A TIME

Poverty Point is the best-known archaeological site in Louisiana.[1] It is a national monument and a World Heritage Site, like other internationally famous places—the Great Pyramids of Egypt, England's Stonehenge and the Great Wall of China. Archaeologists have been working at Poverty Point ever since the first Rex Mardi Gras parade rolled through New Orleans, Pickney Pinchback was governor of Louisiana and Ulysses S. Grant occupied the White House. Several museums, universities, agencies, private firms and unaffiliated individuals have carried out investigations there; among them, the Smithsonian Institution, the American Museum of Natural History, the Academy of Natural Sciences of Philadelphia, the U.S. National Park Service, the U.S. Army Corps of Engineers, the U.S. Army Research and Development Center, the U.S. Soil Conservation Service, the Louisiana Office of State Parks and the Louisiana Division of Archaeology, as well as universities from Alabama, Indiana, Kentucky, Louisiana, Minnesota, Mississippi, Missouri and Ohio. Private firms such as New World Research Inc., Carved Trowel Archaeology Ltd., Cultural Resource Analysts Inc. and J.E. Chance & Associates Inc. have added to the findings, as have staff archaeologists, state regional archaeologists stationed at Poverty Point and friends of Poverty Point, namely Carl Alexander, Michael Beckman, James Marshall and Clarence Webb.

Poverty Point Legends & Lore is not about these investigations, discoveries or archaeological theories. It does not dwell on earthen architecture or handicrafts or on lifeways or living history. This book focuses on a different dimension, the spectral dimension of Poverty Point. While scientific types may scoff at the suggestion that anything other than natural agency is responsible for the strange and unusual events recounted herein, there is no denying that these accounts constitute a rich body of folklore best appreciated around a crackling campfire or atop Mound B under the stars. What animates many of the narratives is the correspondence with characters and events in the old stories told by the Choctaw Natives and neighboring southern tribes.[2] Complementing these traditional stories are snippets about other strange or inexplicable incidents and vignettes of human interest.

Many stories originated with the stream of archaeologists and university students who have been spending summers at Poverty Point since it opened as a State Commemorative Area in 1975. Archaeological field schools were the prevalent venue for the stories, as well as the main propagators. Field schools were basically excavation training programs, but they quickly became mobile, close-knit communities by semesters' ends. Individuals enrolled; family left.

We conducted eight field schools at Poverty Point, in 1983, 1985, 1988, 1989, 1991, 1993, 1995 and 1998 (see acknowledgements). In addition, we also held annual spring equinoctial field trips, or pilgrimages. Most ULL students were anthropology majors or had worked with me on other archaeological excavations or ongoing lab work during the course of the school year. For the most part, participants were already immersed in Poverty Point matters, were excavation-tempered and were ready and anxious to wield a trowel.

There was always pervasive excitement about pending field schools, especially after the previous year's returning class shared their stories of good times, intrigue and magic. Back at the university, prerequisite courses filled quickly, especially classes on archaeological field methods and Louisiana Natives. Volunteers helped with ongoing lab work and artifact analyses. Veterans of previous digs signed on to help with upcoming schools. Even now, long after our last Poverty Point field school, veterans still bring their children and grandchildren to Poverty Point to show them where they found some memorable artifact or saw the spirit fox, and they tell them the old stories.

Poverty Point's physical facilities were built with archaeological research in mind—a museum, working laboratory, water-screening station, theater for lectures, site manager's cottage, artifact storage facility and coed dormitory with guest rooms and sleeping quarters, kitchen, bathrooms/showers,

Right: "Now, when you get to be big archaeologists this tall…"—Top trowel gives opening instructions, while Kerry wonders what he's gotten himself into. *Photograph by Danielle Bacque*

Below: A tiny red jasper owl pendant, also known as the Robinson owl, after its lucky discoverer. *Photograph by Donna Trahan.*

laundry room and commons area. All of the amenities are those of a first-rate, self-contained, on-site research facility. Adding ambiance to this layout was the dorm's location, hidden away in the peaceful woods along Harlin Bayou, far from the comings and goings of school buses, RVs and vehicles with out-of-state plates.

It was a different story during the workday. Our digs were deemed part of Poverty Point's interpretative program, so park staff would lead tram-loads of tourists or parties of hikers to view our excavations. We would display some of our daily finds and have one of our silver-tongued emissaries explain what was going on. One memorable account came in response to a tourist's question about what we had found that morning. "Oh, just four or five projectile points, a figurine and a couple a' those red jasper owls…but they're bagged up in the lab right now," dead-panned Tribbey.[3] Shortly thereafter, park rangers started delivering those pit-side updates themselves, giving us more hands in the pits, I believe was Dennis's courteous explanation.

Field school was organized around a series of activities, and students cycled through all of them. Everybody spent time mapping, excavating and doing lab work. Everybody pulled KP duty (including breakfast, lunch and supper—kitchen cleanup only—supper meal was prepared by hired cooks) and dorm housekeeping (including cleaning toilets), and everybody attended evening lectures by guest speakers, usually held once or twice weekly. The daily routine began with reveille at 5:30 a.m.; followed by breakfast at 6:00 a.m.; a walk to the assigned work site, arriving by 7:00 a.m.; work; a thirty-minute lunch break; work a little more; knock off at 2:30 p.m., before afternoon heat strokes; walk back to the dorm; catnap; shower; supper at 5:30 p.m.; weekly lectures; and then happy hours with mates or nightly communion with the spirits.

Comments personalize the routine:

> *My husband says, "Let's get this straight. You're choosing to go up there to dig in the dirt, do KP duty and clean toilets."—Kay*[4]

> *We were up at 5:30 every morning, except for K.B., who was up at 4:45 to make breakfast.—Anonymous (note: Breakfast included her scrumptious cat-back biscuits.—J.L.G.)*

> *Who needs milk of magnesia? Just swallow a little bit of loess.—Arville*[5]

Through hands eternal—"Peas" and "Carrots" hold a hematite plummet found in a North Three test pit. *Photograph by Danielle Bacque.*

There, on the bank of Bayou Macon, we said goodbye to the site, the ancients, and each other. We thanked the ancients once again and walked very slowly down the path that led us out of the shaded woods into the bright sunlight.—Lynn

May 18: There is a kinda awesome feeling in the woods where we're digging. Sorta like someone is watching you.—Mark

May 19: I kept mopping myself into corners—nothing like a little housework to make you feel stupid.—Ashleigh

May 19: In level 1, we found a hematite plummet—yeah—it's absolutely beautiful.—Shelly

May 19: Everyone told me I had to write in this book—I can't, I'm too damn tired.—Ruby (Brought Ruby a straw to drink her beer when she is exhausted.—Ellen)

May 19: 10:35 a.m., Carl K. told us that we shouldn't walk on the pit floor if we didn't have to: "If you start off with a bad pit, you'll end up with a bad pit."—Greg

May 20: Finally got my trowel dirty. Dug level 5. Took about one and a half hours.—Patricia

May 20: I was worried about poison ivy; no problem, but so far, been bitten by everything but a rat snake.—Danielle

May 25: 6:30 a.m. cleanup duties (unfortunately, my partner admits she doesn't know how to mop).—Cathy (Another anonymous student was overheard asking Gloria how she could tell when water boiled—J.L.G.)

May 26: Mapping with Rachelle and Debra. Doing fill-in points for contour map, 287 degrees. Got to hold stadia rod, a pain in the ass for us short people to read while holding.—Leslie

May 31: I absolutely love telling the story of this place with a map. —Rachelle

May 31: Weighed PPOs most of the day—thank God we don't have to count the suckers.—Azar

May 31: The variation in the soil is really becoming apparent now—very beautiful. One can begin to get a sense of actions of the past—movement… even of time passed.—Shelly

June 1: Pit has been officially closed. We went down 14 levels, nearly a meter and a half. Our walls look so nice. I'm proud of our pit—[I know] that sounds funny.—Nicole

June 5: Clean up after dinner. I think we have washed every pot, fork, and cup twice today.—Tara

June 6: The last part of the day was spent collecting things such as string from the test pits or a handful of dirt from the last level so everyone could remember the experience. Along with my souvenir test pit string, I've decided to take Doc's Chevy pickup.—Greg

June 6: 1:00 p.m.—finished all profiles and waiting on the truck to bring Doc's stick for the closing ceremony. Without the stakes and string, our pit looks like a big hole in the ground. It's a little strange to look at it now. Maybe that's because it's over, but we don't have closure yet. Not quite able to let go. The stick is here now.—Liz

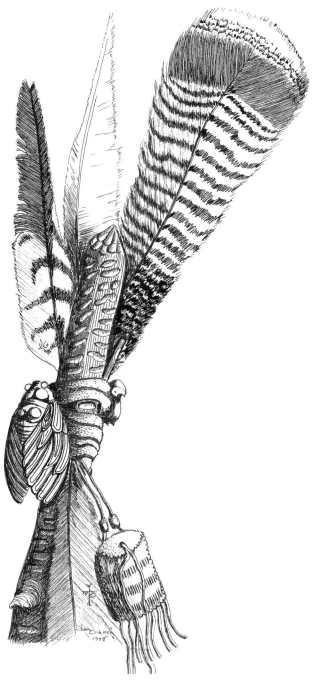

The Stick, an adorned beaver-gnawed branch used to ceremonially "heal"
our disturbances in anthropic earth by pledging to faithfully record findings in
remembrance of the Ancients. *Drawn by Jon Gibson.*

June 6: We laid our pit…to rest today. [Doc] *healed the wound in the earth with his beaver stick.…I was moved by the ceremony but needed to have the umbilical with my pit officially severed.*—*Ted*

Unless otherwise attributed, the preceding remarks from student field books were previously printed in *Cool Dark Woods, Poison Ivy, and Maringoins: The 1993 Excavations at Poverty Point* and in *By the Shining Bayou Waters: The 1995 Excavations at Poverty Point.*[6]

Usually, by the time the bottom bunks had been claimed and the first sit-down supper had been taken together, the family had begun forming, and by dig's end, you would've thought Spock had died again, judging from the teary eyes and long hugs.

Repeated exposure to Native oral narratives and Poverty Point's rich iconography and architectural embodiments, coupled with extended stays in the rural Louisiana outback, where abundant wildlife and black nights move to a different rhythm, heightened sensory awareness and made the impossible seem possible—even likely. At Poverty Point, it becomes easy to envision a hoot owl morphing into a *shilombish*, a singing locust becoming a red jasper pendant or even a human with a full red beard turning into the fox-man, a transformation I dreamed I witnessed one dark night at the crater near the Great Mound.[7] With every retelling, these stories take on a life and credibility of their own.

Versions of some of these stories were included in limited distribution reports of excavations printed by the Center for Archaeological Studies at the University of Southwestern Louisiana. They are rewritten here. For the most part, they are being retold as originally presented, with only minor editing, clarifications and reference additions. They faithfully preserve conversations that I participated in, or overheard firsthand or were reported to me shortly after the precipitating occasion. My direct involvement explains why many of these stories are recounted in the first person. Passages from students' field books reminded me of other situations and exchanges. For still other previously unrecorded or briefly mentioned incidents, elaborated herein for the first time, I reproduce conversations as closely as I remember them from two to four decades ago. Where licenses have been taken, they involve lapses in these aged memories or in cleansing the vernacular, but regardless of whether verbal exchanges are reproduced verbatim or not, the gist of the supplied conversation is essentially faithful to the contexts and personalities involved.

Another reporting convention—to shield participants' identities, I only use their given names or nicknames, even in cases where two people bear the same name. They will be able to recognize themselves and others from the circumstances. Full names are used when acknowledging an author of a published reference.

In keeping with the familiar tenor of the book, I only cite essential literature. Readers seeking more comprehensive information may wish to consult the bibliography and suggested readings.

1

POVERTY POINT, AN ARCHAEOLOGICAL DIGEST

Poverty Point is located near the Mississippi River in upper northeastern Louisiana. Between 1680 and 1170 cal. BCE (dates calibrated with Calib 7.10 protocols, using IntCal13 terrestrial data), Poverty Point was home to a large group of Natives who constructed a gigantic earthwork on the grounds, the largest ever constructed in prehistoric Louisiana and one of the largest in mainland North America.

Ruins of this ancient town cling to the bluff-lined edge of a forested massif rising out of the Mississippi River swampland. Viewed from above, today, the ruins form a giant crescent-shaped figure consisting of six concentric earthen embankments, or elevated rings. The rings encircle the remains of a dismantled woodhenge and ditch. Two paralleling, mound-appointed ley lines flank the figure. Household debris caps the embankments and is scattered over small rises throughout the immediately surrounding countryside. Several coeval villages and scores of camps lie deeper in the hinterland.

EARTHWORK

For nearly five centuries, residents labored on the earthwork. They paid tribute to the ancestors by using a standing mound built 1,500 years earlier as the starting point for a covert way leading to the new construction site, which lay to the north immediately alongside an old torn-down woodhenge.

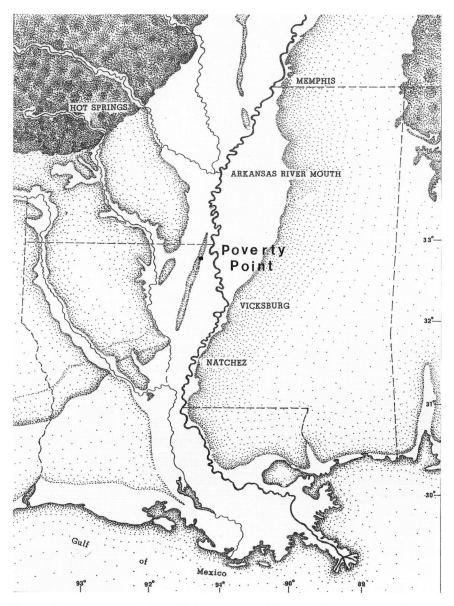

Poverty Point sits on a wooded massif rising above the Mississippi River swampland in northeastern Louisiana. *Drawn by Jon Gibson.*

Busy resident workers construct earthen rings. *Drawn by Jon Gibson.*

This virtual primary way line ran northward for more than 3,465 meters (or 40 basic architectural units) to a viewpoint where the winter solstice sun could be seen rising in the southeastern sky, over a stomp ground or a ritual structure (a spot that, after being capped many times, became the Dunbar, or Plaza, Mound). The sun-designated intersection and the stomp ground waypoint were located 568 meters apart (a distance that equals 13 halved basic architectural units).[8] At this viewpoint, around 1628 cal. BCE, workers erected a knee-high earthen platform, which they periodically capped on at least six ensuing occasions. The final addition was not leveled but was left as a pile of dirt, which changed the overall shape from a flat-topped platform to a conical form (Mound B).

Despite the generation-spanning, stop-and-start or progressive construction, planners still managed to integrate cosmic- or ceremonial-cycle equivalents into the ever-expanding earthwork by lengthening or shortening the distance between mounds. After erecting the inaugural mound (Mound B), they raised additional mounds along parallel or perpendicular vectors, which were laid off by means of virtual three-four-five-proportional triangulation. They measured distance with something like a human chain or a knotted cord with knots tied at arm span intervals. After fifteen or so generations, they had constructed six or possibly seven mounds and a series of six concentric raised rings.

An arm span seems to have been the standard unit of measure; it is the closest anatomical equivalent to 1.67 meters, which is the only mathematical factor inherent in mound dimensions and inter-mound distances that yields the full slate of day-count cycles found in Native cosmic numerology, including 13, 18, 20, 52, 260, 360 and 364–65 day counts.[9]

The old Choctaw people even had a word for the arm-span distance when speaking of the relationship between fire, especially the sacred temple fire and the sun, considered their supreme spirit.

> *In ancient times, fire, as the most striking representation of the sun, was considered as possessing intelligence and as acting in concert with the sun. The fire and sun were supposed to have constant intercourse with each other, and the fire acted the part of an informant to the sun. And it was an ancient saying of theirs, that if one did anything wrong in the presence of the fire, the fire would tell the sun of it before the offender could go ashatapa, the length of his extended arms.*[10]

In a bird's eye—Poverty Point showing earthwork in its final form around 1170 BCE. *Drawn by Jon Gibson.*

Clearly, the old mound-building Choctaw people saw the relationship between the arm span, the sacred fire (the earth-bound representation of the sun) and the sun on high. The shared mathematics inherent in Archaic and Poverty Point earthworks reveals just how long Native peoples have been looking to the cosmos, particularly the sun, for their manifest spiritual inspiration.

The basic architectural unit was fifty-two arm spans long, a distance of eighty-six and two-thirds meters by today's reckoning, a value equivalent to four solar years among some Lower Mississippi tribes, such as the Natchez. The Natchez year consisted of thirteen named "moons," so four years is the linear equivalent of fifty-two moons. This same cycle is also represented in earlier Archaic earthen architectural dimensions, as well as in the later Yucatec Maya calendar.[11]

These equivalencies were built into the construction process from the onset and did not materialize only at completion, and this negates claims that builders had followed a preset grand design from the beginning. What actually transpired was progressive construction wherein each new mound or ring was linked to the founding solar-positioned structure in an ever-expanding network laid off by right triangulation. Distances between mounds and rings were the linear equivalent of the number of days in the ceremonial cycle being celebrated by each newly initiated structure, cycles such as a solar or tropical year, a lunar maximum, or a forty-day transit of the sun along the horizon (the Yucatec Maya's "Footprint of the Year").

DOMESTIC AND POLITICAL ECONOMY

Poverty Point's domestic economy, once presumed to be based on maize or native seed cultivation, has since has been found to be a unique kind of stilled wild food and fishing-collecting strategy, focused on slack-water fish and aquatic roots, supplemented, in season, with logistically exploited upland game, wild seeds, acorns and nuts.[12]

Trace elemental analyses have revealed that the greater share of rock Poverty Point craftspeople used to fabricate their hardware came by way of interconnected rivers, as long suspected, but this has reopened the nagging question of how tons of rock were acquired, whether by direct "mining," long-distance trading or, perhaps, recycling the leftovers of pilgrims from afar.

Poverty Point women dig lotus roots in nearby Joe's Bayou. *Drawn by Jon Gibson.*

Several technological renovations define the onset of Poverty Point culture. In keeping with the growing reliance on aquatic food stuffs and increased earthwork labor demands, Poverty Point cooks devised a more efficient, time-saving cooking facility: the earth oven. Earth ovens were steep-sided conical or cylindrical pits, usually deeper than they were wide. The internal temperature was regulated with small, preheated, hand-molded earthen objects. Called Poverty Point objects, or PPOs, these objects were fashioned into a half dozen or so basic shapes, and these distinctive shapes helped determine how long ovens remained hot.

You probably remember the underlying principle from high school physics—the Stephan-Boltzmann law: hot objects with larger surface areas transfer heat longer than those with less. Practically, this means that foods, such as fish, which didn't take long to cook, could have been baked with a few plain objects, such as bicones; whereas lotus rhizomes were more readily prepared with more complex PPO forms, such as cross-grooved melons or grooved cylinders. Heat transfer stopped when the internal temperature of the food reached the same temperature as that in the oven, so using the right kind of objects meant that there were no more scorched, dried-out or underdone foods, just fully cooked meals, without having an

Above: Preparing food
the Poverty Point way. A
contemporary cookout, an
earth oven heated with PPOs.
Photograph by Jon Gibson.

Right: Poverty Point objects, or
PPOs. Shapes regulated the
cooking temperature in earth
ovens. *Drawn by Jon Gibson.*

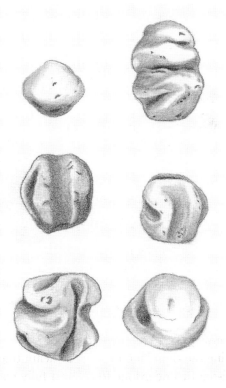

Above: A Poverty Point fisherman running gill net in a flooded swamp. *Drawn by Jon Gibson.*

Left: Plummets, or net weights. When added to mudlines, these heavy weights kept stationary fishnets and seines from rolling up in flooded woods or backwaters while being dragged ashore at a haul bank. *Drawn by Jon Gibson.*

experienced cook constantly add firewood or monitor cooking progress. It was a godsend for people whose workdays were often made busier by having to labor on the mounds. Plus, food stayed warm in the oven until families were ready to eat.

Another domestic-economic improvement involved net fishing technology. Although nets had been used for a long time in the Lower Mississippi Valley, Poverty Point fishermen redesigned them by adding heavy weights to the mudline commonly known as plummets.[13] Plummets kept nets and seines unfurled in a current or while being dragged along a slough or lake bottom. This small change had large repercussions for both the domestic and political economy.

Men of importance—an imaginary scene—a grand headman descends Great Mound on the shoulders of his bearers, preceded by an owl-masked shaman priest. *Drawn by Jon Gibson.*

Weighted nets enabled fishermen to catch fish in all kinds of bodies of water from lakes and flooded swamps to rivers and bayous, but most importantly, they extended the fishing season throughout the whole year, including winter and spring floods. Overcoming these normally austere times meant that people could remain in their home villages year-round without having to seasonally scatter throughout the swampland.

Not only would weighted nets have ensured stability in the home-based mound-building workforce, but they would have enabled greater flexibility in carrying out other essential tasks, including mining or trading ventures to the Ouachita Mountains, where plummet-raw materials were procured, as well more distant mountains for flint, copper, galena and other rocks.

Prestige would have accrued to people involved in these ventures as a consequence of acquiring and sharing desirable materials and simply dealing with strange peoples and exotic places. Status unbalancing in acephalous communities carries a potential for creating social and political unrest and even community fragmentation, and there is compelling circumstantial evidence for political rivalry in the near-simultaneous erection of Poverty Point's two massive mounds so close to the moment of abandonment.[14]

THE SPIRIT WORLD

Another dimension of Poverty Point's daily life that underwent elaboration had to do with the spirit world, particularly its objectification. Poverty Point's materiality harbors a sizeable slate of small symbolic carvings, engravings and architectural forms that portray a panorama of beasts, fowls, chimeras, glyphs and celestial geometry.[15] Among the small stone carvings are realistic fat-bellied owls, bird heads, claws/talons and clam shells, as well as soapstone vessels, geometric objects, bannerstones, gorgets, plummets and beads bearing etchings of crows, panthers, perching birds, nestlings, "long-tails" and turtles (gopher tortoise and stinkpot species). Other engravings include abstract "fox-men" (or perching owl), merged eternities, Grecian keys, skate keys and rain-cloud glyphs.[16]

Virtually the full spectrum of imagery is represented by the characters in traditional oral narratives of historic Southeastern tribes, and they typically relate to the ethereal world of epic tales, culture heroes, spirit beings and magic.[17] For instance, owls are associated with death, souls, witchcraft and seeing at night; other birds are associated with news-bringing, early warnings and kindness. Foxes and fox chimeras are

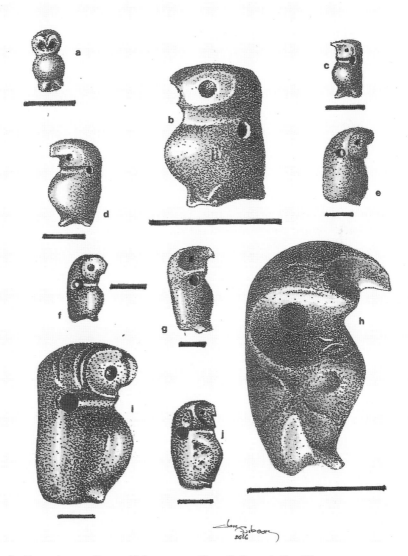

Opposite: Engravings on Poverty Point stone artifacts, I. *Drawn by Jon Gibson.*

Above: Fat-bellied owls. Poverty Point is the inspirational center for these charms or fetishes, which are scattered across the gulf states from western Louisiana to central Florida, possibly following "trail trade" or intervillage visits. All scales equal one centimeter. *Drawn by Jon Gibson.*

Opposite: Engravings on Poverty Point stone artifacts, II. *Drawn by Jon Gibson.*

Right: *Nalusa Falaya*, the long, black being of the Choctaw. *Drawn by Jon Gibson.*

associated with *kashehotapalo*, a combination of human and deer "who delights in frightening hunters," and *nalusa falaya*, "the long black being," who looks like a man "but has small eyes and long, pointed ears and sometimes frightens hunters or even communicates its own power of doing harm."[18] Other possible associations include the panther with "water panther" stories, "long-tail" with opossum stories and glyphs (single-path labyrinths) with "road of life" themes.[19]

It is also evident that Poverty Point's view of the heavens was embedded in architecture. Some earthwork alignments honor solstice sightlines, and dimensions and distances express ceremonial cycles and right-triangle ratio values.[20] Firmament to ground transferal was accomplished by laying off inter-mound distances, which corresponded to day counts in the solar or ceremonial cycle being celebrated (with each day "counted" as a standard length unit equivalent to an arm span (or approximately one and two-third meters in today's metrics). Larger units of measure equivalent to fifty-two arm spans, or eighty-six and two-third meters, formed the basic architectural unit.[21]

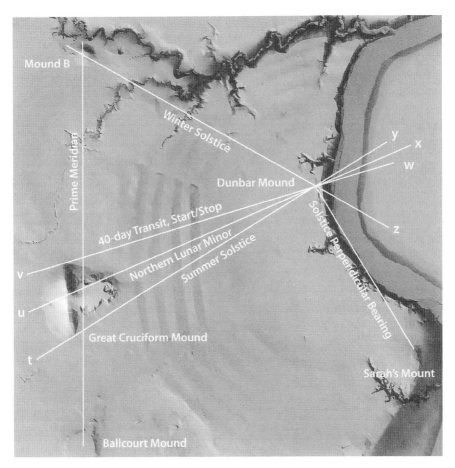

Ceremonial cycles built into Poverty Point earthwork using solstice alignments and inter-mound spacing variances. *Digitally created by Diana Greenlee, adapted from astronomical data provided by Robert Patten and LIDAR base map provided by FEMA and the state of Louisiana and distributed by Atlas: The Louisiana Statewide GIS, LSU CADGIS Research Laboratory, Baton Rouge, courtesy of the University of Louisiana at Monroe.*

Distance-represented cycles discovered in Poverty Point's earthwork include: (a) thirteen cycles, or 568.7 meters, which is the distance between the Plaza Mound (Dunbar Mound) and the conical mound (Mound B) along the winter solstice sightline divided by forty-three and a third meters, or one-half the basic architectural unit; (b) thirteen cycles, also represented by the distance between the Plaza Mound and the summit of the massive western mound (Mound A), the opposite leg of an equilateral triangle with its apex on the Plaza Mound; (c) eighteen (basic architectural unit) cycles or 360 (arm span) cycles, or 600 meters, which is the distance between the two main paralleling ley lines; (d) eight fifty-two (arm span) cycles, or 693 meters, which is the length of the hypotenuse of the two conjoined right triangles used to lay off the paralleling ley lines; and (e) two 260 arm span cycles, or 867 meters, which is the distance between Mound B and a small platform mound (Sarah's Mount) that was placed atop the innermost embankment in the southern part of the crescent.[22]

Identical cycles are represented in Lower Mississippi Archaic earthworks that were built as much as 2,000 years earlier, in addition to comprising the divisions of the Mesoamerican solar calendar 1,500 years later.

Question: Did ancient sky watchers in Louisiana and Mesoamerica independently recognize the same cosmic/ceremonial cycles, as well as the same standard measure, or is there a far more interesting story involving travel adventure, *festivals internationale* and foreign diplomacy? The answer may not be as elusive as it seems. The Mesoamerican building plan incorporates the same basic cycles and trigonometric resolutions as in Louisiana, despite being based on angular regularities that can only be directly observed/resolved at the 31.6 north latitude, which is the precise location of the earliest Louisiana mound group known to harbor cosmic cycles, located only a few miles south of Poverty Point.

TIME'S ARROW

The accelerant behind and the history of Poverty Point, the town and way of life are not fully understood, but one thing is relatively clear: both were interwoven and fast-paced. Around 1628 cal. BCE, local folk started building a mound at the intersection of the winter solstice sightline and a virtual way line running northward from the ancestral genesis mound, clearly establishing Poverty Point's roots in living spiritualism. Over the following years, residents carried out a large-scale building program, including land-leveling and building mounds, raised rings and posted circles. As the population grew, new demands on living and working together ensued. New technologies, practices and institutions ramped up and were integrated with the old-time spiritual tradition predicated on creationism and cosmology. Two long-standing great subdivisions cleaved civil society and codified behaviors between the divisions.

Sometime during the first few decades of the twelfth century BCE (before 1170 BCE), after five hundred years of prosperity and civility, these subdivisions, or at least homegrown antagonists or disgruntled families

Feathered shaman priests from the Motley Mound sect listen to a holy man from a rival Great Mound sect offer prayers to Creator Sun. An imaginary scene during Poverty Point's end of days. *Drawn by Jon Gibson.*

from the first and then the other subdivision, broke with long-standing civil conduct and tradition and pursued adversarial or self-serving agendas or opposing ideologies. Their narcissism and anger culminated in the near-simultaneous erection of Poverty Point's two giant mounds at a high cost in labor, capital, and patronage. The effort was a communal undoing—it slowed and quickly suspended Poverty Point's pioneering effort in grand sedentary living.

"While post-apocalyptic leaders strutted around in their fluffed-up feather capes and painted faces, many, eventually all, folk doused their cooking fires and push-poled their way across the black waters into self-imposed oblivion."[23]

2

STORIES BEARING NATIVE CORRESPONDENCE

Poverty Point is more than a famous archaeological site or a pretty place to have a picnic or take a hike. An indefinable mystique cloaks its grounds, a palatable aura that pervades even the least superstitious among us. Real-life events bear witness, especially when many of them can be related to Native contexts.

THE FALLING TREE INCIDENT

Near the Great Mound, a sweetgum tree crashed to the ground, scattering the group of university students who happened to be walking nearby. Nobody was hurt, but nerves were rattled. Everybody wondered what caused the tree to fall seemingly out of the clear blue sky. The day, after all, was clear and blue—and calm. Apprehension deepened when a veteran of Poverty Point affairs started telling of other strange happenings.

"Y'all come see," Dawn beckoned. "This tree's been struck by lightning before. See the split? That's why it died. It was about ready to fall anyway."

Aha, mystery solved—or was it?

The story of *Mela'tha*, the great lightning bird of the Choctaw, came to mind.

> *Thunder and lightning are to the Choctaw two great birds—Thunder (Heloha), the female; Lightning (Mela'tha), the male. When they hear a*

A tree falls, startling a group of contemporary Poverty Point pilgrims walking past—sign or coincidence? "Just a reminder that welcome we may be—and we are—what we do does not go unnoticed, and what we hold in trust isn't to be taken lightly," said Dawn McCulley Pesnell. *Photograph by Dawn McCulley Pesnell.*

great noise in the clouds, Heloha is laying an egg, "just like a bird," in the cloud, which is her nest. When a tree is shattered the result is said to have been caused by Mela'tha, the male, he being the stronger; but when a tree is only slightly damaged, the effect is attributed to Heloha, the weaker.[24]

Still, why did the tree wait to fall until this particular moment? Was it a delayed reminder from *Mela'tha*?

ENCOUNTER WITH GRASS WATER DROP

Once upon a time, a sizable group of field school students returning from a late-night vigil on the summit of the Great Mound encountered a pocket of bone-numbing cold air after hearing an owl hoot. Covered in chill-bumps, they ran all the way back to the dormitory, where the night air was pleasant. Several brave boys thought they had seen a light moving through the trees ahead of them like a big unblinking eye.

"Awh, that was only a localized temperature inversion," reasoned a know-it-all.

"That wasn't no eye, neither," added his buddy, grinning. "Jus' the spotlight of that local yokel who's been patrolling out here every night. Right, Doc?"

"Who knows," I said, even while thinking about the story of *Hashok Okwa Hui'ga*, or "Grass Water Drop," the Choctaw will-o'-the-wisp, who can only be seen at night and then only its glowing heart is visible.[25] I thought it best not to mention that the Choctaw believed the hooting of *opa*, the barred owl, portended the death of a close relative.[26] There was no sense adding more anxiety, especially when hooting owls provide nightly taps at Poverty Point.

"You know, you said it felt just like somebody opened the door of a refrigerator," said Fogie, looking up from the Bourré table. "Well, did you ever think it might have been a portal from some icy parallel dimension, just like they showed on *Twilight Zone* the other night?"

"Come on, Fogie, it's your play," said Ann. "You're getting delusional again."

HALLEY'S COMET AND THE MIST

In March and April 1986, Halley's comet was clearly visible in the night sky. We were at Poverty Point on our annual pilgrimage held to celebrate the vernal equinox and choose a location for our upcoming summer dig. Several pilgrims decided to get up in the wee hours of the morning and hike to Sarah's Mount, where the view of the comet would be unimpeded

A comet in the sky above Poverty Point. Bennet's Comet, taken from the plaza, sixty-second timed exposure, March 21, 1970. *Photograph by Carl Alexander.*

by the surrounding woods. The night was moonless, and the sky was starry, ensuring good visibility, but just as we glimpsed the comet from atop Sarah's Mount, a thick mist streamed out of the deep gully beside the mound, obscuring everything. Everyone was unnerved. We hurried back toward the dormitory, but before we had gone one hundred yards, someone nervously said, "Y'all better turn around and look, the fog's gone."

Nobody wanted to return to the mound, but they all decided to observe the comet from the tree-shrouded dormitory parking lot, which, of course, they couldn't, but then, they already knew that. At the time, I marked up the fast-moving mist as one of those strange events that happens so often at Poverty Point.

Some weeks later, while preparing a lecture on Choctaw cosmology, I came across this: "Great trouble or even war was supposed to follow the sight of a comet."[27] Had the mist averted great trouble in our gathering that night by hiding the comet? I don't know, but we didn't get to view the comet, and we didn't experience any trouble.

Our First Day Is Going to Be Our Last

The first day of the first excavation season I ever held at Poverty Point was June 3, 1983. The morning dawned innocently enough, although it was unusually warm, with a blustery southwesterly breeze. The survey crew was in the middle of setting up the plane table and alidade when we noticed that the magnetic needle kept bouncing from side to side instead of coming to rest due north.

"We're gonna have to move. We're too close to the high wires," said Wade.

That's when the sky darkened, the temperature dropped and marble-sized hail started falling. Dust and leaves blew hard out of the southwest, and a blue aura enveloped the instrument. Ears popped, and the hair on our arms stood up in the static electricity. We looked up into the swirling vortex of a funnel cloud passing directly overhead. "Oh, lordy," I thought, "Our first day is going to be our last."

After silent prayers and regaining our feet, we watched the tornado touch down a few hundred yards away, tearing a path through the cotton and destroying the Morning Star Baptist Church before lifting into the angry black cloud that spawned it.

Just as suddenly as it materialized, it was gone. The needle found north, and life resumed.

Later that summer, I looked to no avail through my books for some Lower Mississippi tribal story having to do with

A rain cloud glyph. An abstract engraving on bannerstone, possibly depicting a driving rain or hail-producing storm. *Drawn by Jon Gibson.*

tornados and damaging winds. Nothing sounded relevant, so I reasoned that some occurrences at Poverty Point must have natural explanations.

On second thought, nawh.

BLACKSNAKES AND KENTUCKY FRIED CHICKEN

Once upon a time, several families were eating at the picnic tables near the museum. Our field school was digging on one of the western embankments about a quarter of a mile away when we suddenly heard the picnickers yelling and saw them running around.

"What you think is going on?" asked "Gnat." "You reckon they need help?"

"Nawh, there comes Dennis's truck," said John, as the park superintendent's pickup raced toward the excited crowd.

Dennis jumped out, spoke with the tall man and strode toward the tables. People were milling around excitedly, and some adults kept pointing up into the big oak tree that shaded the tables. Dennis walked back toward the tall man, who was shaking his head. Obviously disgruntled, the tall man threw up his hands. The crowd hurriedly packed up the food and ice chests and headed toward the parking lot. We watched as Dennis climbed back into his pickup and headed across the plaza toward our dig area.

"Biggest dadgum snake I ever saw," said Dennis, grinning just like he just heard a Boudreaux and Thibodaux joke. "There were two of 'em. The little one's still up in the fork of the oak, but the big one fell out of the tree, landed on the table, smack dab in the middle of their Kentucky Fried Chicken. Reckon they musta' been, uh, you know, mating or something."

Dennis unwrapped his Swisher Sweet and bit off the end before continuing. "Anyway, them folks wanted a shovel so they could kill the big one that landed in their chicken, but I told them they couldn't. Then they wanted me to kill it and get the other one down from the tree. I told them, no, that we didn't kill snakes here, they're protected because they're part of the park's natural environment."

Dennis paused, putting the cigar back in the holder in his shirt pocket. "Well, let me tell you, they sure didn't want to hear that. They said this was a public picnic area, and I was supposed to keep it safe. They said they were leaving and would *not* be coming back. Oh well, that's the way it goes sometimes," Dennis reasoned, climbing in his truck.

As he was leaving, Dennis hung his head out of the pickup window and shouted: "Hey, y'all gonna have to call this the 'Season of the Snake.'"

And so, it came to be.

By the way, the snakes were black rat snakes, creme bellies and uniformly black backs—blacksnakes. Smithsonian ethnologist John Swanton notes: "They [the Choctaw] claimed that though the blacksnake would not harm anyone, it would try to scare a person."[28]

We can say with certainty that it succeeded.

GATORS AND THE ARTIFACT HUNTERS

We heard the low, deep-throated roar before the first shovelful of silt loam passed through the screen. But curiosity was overcome quickly by the excitement of the opening day of excavation at the world-famous Poverty Point site. Then, too, there was the further excitement of gender comingling among healthy adults from the three participating universities, whose lives for the next several weeks were going to be spent in the cozy confines of one-by-one-meter test pits. An hour later, the blazing sun had calmed the collective excitement, and somebody noticed the low roar again.

"You think that's a bullfrog?"

"*Mais non, cher*, not in dis heat," said Arville knowingly. "Dey holler for rain and in de dark."

At that moment, one of Jack's survey team members who was busy laying off additional test pits along the lip of the "Dock" called out, "You guys better come see these alligators, they're monsters."

Everyone dropped their trowels and shovels and raced to the top of the Dock, fascinated by the two reptiles sunning on the muddy bayou bank at the foot of the Dock. One was a goliath ten-footer; the other was smaller, about seven or eight feet long.

"I've never seen a real alligator before," said one of the Akronites.

"Heck," said Tribbey, "they're so common where we're from, we've even got them on campus. Somebody said they ate a student a few years ago, and they're always finding swan feathers and chewed-up dog collars around the lake at the student union."

"Awh, Tribbey, be quiet. Somebody's gonna believe you."

After the initial encounter, the 'gators simply blended into Poverty Point's background, just like cypress trees, fire ants and stirrings after dark. Small knots of students did pass by the 'gator dens after work and congregate atop the Dock at noon while eating their peanut-butter-and-jelly sandwiches.

I kept watch, too—furtively—not wishing to show too much concern but also not wanting a careless close-up photographer to become a tasty morsel on my watch. In addition, Mitchell and I had trot lines set in several honey holes near the 'gator dens, and we knew quite well that alligators liked Opelousa catfish as much as we did. There was no need to lose an arm trying to untangle a line.

Alligators had not been seen in Bayou Macon for many years, so these reptiles were clearly a spectacle. One day, Wendell, my old college roommate, drove over from Jackson to visit. He explained why the 'gators were there, and if anyone would know, it was Wendell. He was an endangered species biologist for the U.S. Fish and Wildlife Service and had spent years studying alligators.

We were catching up in the shade of a big oak tree on the Dock, watching the largest beast toss garfish into a water-filled hole he had wallowed out in the bank. Several garfish were already swimming around in his homemade live well.

"Good," I thought, "maybe he won't have the *envies* for human morsels."

Test pits laid out on "Turtle Nest," a food-preparation and outdoor dining area at the northern end of the Dock. *Photograph by Lisa Coleman.*

Wendell explained that these were rogue males seeking new territories. Sometimes, he continued, homeless males will walk for miles overland in their quest for female companions, "just like we used to do at Northwestern."

For the next three weeks, the 'gators basked in the sun and reduced the gar population in the bayou. We kept watch and nervously wondered where they were when they were out of sight.

The last day of the dig came, and many of the students walked down to the water's edge to take pictures of the 'gators. They were nowhere to be seen, and we learned later that they had left for good. Curious thing, huh? 'gators moving in on the first day of the 1988 field season and leaving the day before we did. Some might prefer to call this a coincidence.

It's odd that Native stories about alligators are relatively uncommon among tribes from the Lower Mississippi and Gulf Coastal regions, where 'gators were most prevalent, and those that were told usually involved Native hunters. One Choctaw story relates how a luckless deer hunter helped a thirsty alligator get back to water, and in return, the alligator taught the hapless hunter how to be successful.[29] Were the 'gators attending field school to ensure that our hunt would be successful? Who really knows, but then ask yourself if you believe in coincidences.

DANCING RABBITS AND THE CAUSEWAY

It was the late spring of 1983, right after we regained our composure following the tornado incident. The field crew under Ed's, Wade's and Fogie's capable supervision was busy digging in the Plaza Mound, a mound that Clarence Moore called Mound E and Ford and Webb discounted because locals claimed it was a Confederate cannon redoubt.[30] Wishing to avoid the confusion of having to change the lettering every time a new mound was discovered or an old one was discredited, we decided to christen the structure Dunbar Mound after an escaped turtle, which was to have become the main ingredient of a sauce piquante. Somehow, Dunbar, the turtle, managed to climb out of the bed of Wade's old blue Dodge pickup, the "Blue Goose," where he was being held, and was making his way across the mound, bound for the safety of the bayou, when he was recaptured. In view of his valiant escape attempt, he was granted freedom in a one-sided vote of the crew.

Burney and I heard the cheering but suppressed our curiosity in order to continue preparing the Causeway trench for profiling. Burney was the highway archaeologist for the Arkansas Department of Transportation and an old friend. He was at Poverty Point to give a talk to the crew and help out for a couple of days.

The Causeway was an earthen "bridge" across a natural depression lying just outside the southwestern rings.[31] Local scuttlebutt claimed it was a road that had been built by a residential family to move cattle from their pens to the pasture, but I had doubts. To settle the issue, Big Robert brought the park's backhoe and dug a trench across the feature, the trench where we were then standing knee-deep in water and snakes.

We tossed the snakes out of the trench and bailed—and bailed some more. I trowel-shaved the walls while Burney climbed up the sloping end of the trench and set up the graph paper for profiling. I ran the string line and studied the vivid stratigraphy, which was, from the outset, clearly aboriginal.

Burney pushed his old beat-up felt hat back on his head and called down, "OK, let's do it. Gimme 'em depths every twenty centimeters, Cowboy."

I started pulling tape and calling out measurements when I noticed shadows "flying" over the trench above my head. "Burney, what's with the shadows? Buzzards coming to get you?"

"I don't see any shadows."

"Well, take off that darn hat, and maybe you can see. Look, there's one right now."

Burney stood up. It was a minute before his insistent whisper reached my ears. "Get up here, right now. You gotta see this."

Romping across the sunlit embankments and spilling into the plaza were rabbits, maybe thirty, forty or more. They had been jumping over the trench, casting shadows. We watched, spellbound. Many were standing on their hind legs and pawing at the air with their front legs like boxers jabbing at a speed bag. Others were running around in circles and hopping over each other, while some were loudly stomping their hind feet and making nasal sounds. Then we spotted the object of their undivided affection, and she was hopping away at breakneck speed, heading for the briar patch in the deep gully near Sarah's Mount, her legion of suitors in hot pursuit.

"Son-of-a-gun," Burney proclaimed, "never saw anything like that before. Let's go get a cold one."

"Sounds good to me. We need to get this on the tape recorder, anyway. Nobody's going to believe us."

"You know, when I was working at Pine Bluff, there was a Dancing Rabbit Creek near campus, and seems like I remember something about a treaty or something named after dancing bunnies. Nawh, never mind. That was a Playboy club."

Oral narratives are deafeningly silent about rabbits' stomp dance, although rabbit stories are numerous and widespread among Southeastern tribal peoples.[32] Everywhere, rabbits were tricksters, mischief-makers, liars and schemers. The ubiquity of their rascally character and the wide spread nature of rabbit stories bear witness to great antiquity, to a dim time before many languages and Southern tribes had separated from a common background. The secular nature of rabbits points to the tales being told for childhood amusement rather than for sacred, inspirational or educational purposes. There is little doubt, however, that rabbit folklore fostered tribal togetherness and helped preserve tribal tradition.

One thing is for sure: at Poverty Point, rabbits certainly amused.

Bakbak and the Chosen Test Pit, Part 1

For nearly two decades, I have named the Poverty Point field and laboratory seasons. Usually, the names are derived from the appearance of one of Poverty Point's totem animals on some auspicious occasion or from the occasion itself. Sometimes, the importance of these occasions was not immediately apparent, but not this year. As soon as I opened the door to the dormitory, I found a green-and-yellow-speckled kingsnake on the welcome mat. I shooed him out the back door with a broom before unpacking and paying my respects to the sacred tree.

Since our last field season was named the Season of the Snake, I needed to find another name.[33] I didn't have to wait long. In fact, it presented itself two mornings later at the groundbreaking ceremony on May 18, my mother's birthday.

For nearly two hours, I paced back and forth among the test pits we had staked off on the fifth embankment in the northern sector of the enclosure, waiting for a sign to show me where to take the first shovel of dirt. Which one? I felt no special attraction for any of them. Students were getting persnickety, wondering what was happening. Finally, I picked up a shovel and walked up to a test pit.

"OK, everybody," I summoned, "gather around. I want to say a few words."

I began an opening harangue. I always hold a formal groundbreaking to let students know how serious it is to dig, to willfully disturb the record of the past and to realize how important it is to dutifully record all they can for science and to honor the memory of the old ones.

Kay and Ted string off a test pit. It's supposed to be square when you pull 141.4 centimeters. *Photograph by Danielle Bacque.*

I paused. Other than a noisy blue jay in the distance, there was quiet. Even the trees seemed to be listening. In that moment, I saw all my old Poverty Point friends—Mitchell, Carl, Stu and Clarence. Jim was there, too. I put the blade of the shovel to the ground inside the string-outlined test unit, when suddenly, the silence was shattered by a flutter of wings.

A black-white-and-red flash alit on a small red oak next to unit 5720/5170 and began a staccato drumming. A red-headed woodpecker had flown right into the midst of two dozen people and started searching for bugs just like we weren't there. Did it not see us, or was this *bakbak*, the red-headed sentinel of the Choctaw, the bird that carried news to the villages, announced ballgames and warned war parties of impending danger?[34]

The moment was powerful. Everyone was affected. I had picked the right test pit for the grand opening after all. This was the sign I sought. The season would have its name. Henceforth, it would be called the Season of *Bakbak*, the red-headed woodpecker.

Bakbak and the Chosen Test Pit, Part 2

A second account of the story was penned by eye-witness John Calhoun. His abridged version follows.

It is a solemn moment, a holy one, a ceremony I have witnessed several times over the last eight years, and on each occasion, the import has increased in value through understanding to the point that emotional gestalt is imminent....

Traditionally, Jon breaks ground in his excavations. I have watched him clandestinely for two hours, waiting for him to be ready, to move toward the tool box and select a shovel, as his students are lectured to and learn to string test pits, and I and my help survey a line for more test units....It is a quiet, anxious moment when Jon selects his shovel. A red-headed woodpecker... passes overhead, flies down the line I am surveying, circles an oak once, and disappears, unnoticed, or nearly so.

A hush falls over the site, as all seem to realize that something profound is about to take place. Jon moves to the selected test pit. The woodpecker circles again and lands in the oak, its sabre-like bill pointed at us...then flies south. It is a sign.

Jon's hands rest on the shovel. He speaks of the woodpecker as a sign and pauses....In that pause, Jon, too, has gone south, into the past. He will speak of the ancients and charge these young people with the heavy responsibility of paying attention to detail, not to let a single scrap of understanding slip through their fingers or the screens.

[T]he vision I perceive from his words holds more than ancient hands molding loess cooking balls. I see the ancient one, the one who wears the mask of the fox, was addressed and answered to the name Shaman, who... conveyed more than we are yet ready to understand, and spoke in riddles— always, riddles that make us seek deeper into ourselves for obvious answers that are seldom obvious.

I can feel the yellow-muzzled lips pull back in a fox smile...at Jon's admonishments...and [grasp] that we are here to dig, to seek, to learn, and to come [a] step closer to understanding.[35]

WALKING THE LOG

High Ho, Tippy Toe…
Walking the log,
Just a-walking the log,
If you don't know how to do it,
I'll show you how to walk the log

—adapted from Rufus Thomas's 1963 hit song "Walking the Dog"

The log spanned Harlin Bayou near its junction with Bayou Macon. The treefall happened long ago, and the slumped section of bank that brought down the tree was overgrown with mutton cane and dewberry briars. The twenty-five-foot-high walls of the bayou channel were too steep to climb, and exposed roots and vines dangled over the edge like ancient gnarled fingers of a coven of witches. Midden dirt, black as coffee grounds, was visible in the upper three or four feet of the south bank, where the bayou was actively undercutting the outermost ring of the enclosure (North Five). Fragments of clay balls and flint chips littered the quicksand at the bottom of the chasm and shimmered through the narrow ribbon of clear water spilling into the muddy Bayou Macon.

The northern rings, where we planned to dig this field season, lay on the opposite side of Harlin Bayou, directly across from the dorm where Mitchell and I were contemplating the mysteries of life from the vantage point of our lawn chairs. "Sure wish we could cross the log instead of having to walk around by the road," I said. "It'd save us at least thirty minutes every day, going and coming."

"Yep, but somebody'd fall off and break a bone or worse," drawled Mitchell. "You know, you wouldn't want the kids to walk the log every day, but it might be a good idea to have them cross it right off the bat. That'd be the quickest way to get 'em to work together, make 'em solve a mutual problem."

"Yep, makes sense—no ropes, no ladders, right."

The next morning, just after first light, Mitchell and Carl led the students through the cane and briars to the fallen tree, damp from morning fog and slippery with raccoon scat. I waited on the opposite bank. I had taken the long way around.

"Mornin' y'all. Come on over, and let's get this dig cranked up."

"Doc, how are we supposed to get over there," lamented Debra.

"Oh, you'll find a way. Come on, now, the red owls are waiting."

Mitchell and Carl slid down the steep slope, crept around the tree's root ball, and, arms flailing, successfully walked across the debarked log spanning the bayou.

"OK, Ashleigh, your turn."

With deep breaths taken, thirty young people walked across the log. There was only one casualty, and Charles let us quickly know that he didn't really fall but simply lost his balance and jumped onto the muddy bank below. The problem was that the mud was calf-deep, and he had to use a tree branch as a crutch to navigate through the mire. Henceforth, he proclaimed himself as the official spotter for the group.

With the log crossed, everyone, including mud-caked Charles, gathered on the narrow shelf where the treetop had lodged.

"Now, all we've got to do is figure out how to get up El Capitan here," said Darrel. "Anybody got any ideas?"

Five minutes later, the problem was solved. The small promontory jutted from the bank within an arm length of the exposed roots of an undermined blackgum tree. Using their Marshalltown trowels, the youngsters cut a half dozen toe-hold niches alongside the dangling roots, and *presto*, they had a makeshift ladder, complete with flexible wooden railings. Clinging to the roots, they passed their backpacks up the bank. With university footballers Troy, James and Sean pulling, pushing and cheerleading, the rest of the group climbed or was hoisted to the top of the bank without mishap. The family had been jump-started.

"Well, looks like we made it to the 'Promised Land,'" beamed Debra. "Do we all get As now?"

"Gotta get your trowel dirty before you get grades, Debra," I muttered.

Her comment reminded me of Choctaw chief Peter Pitchlynn's account of souls entering the afterworld.

> [I]*t* [the soul] *arrives at a great chasm in the earth, on the other side of which is the land of the blessed, where there is eternal spring and hunting grounds supplied with great varieties of game. But there is no other means of crossing the fearful gulf but by means of a barked pine log* [a sweetgum log in other versions of the story] *that lies across the chasm, which is round, smooth and slippery. Over this, the disembodied spirits must pass if they are to reach the land of a blissful immortality. Such as have lived purely and honestly upon earth are enabled to pass safely over the terrific abyss on the narrow bridge to the land of happiness.*[36]

Wielding the tools of the trade—three-meter tape and line level. *Photograph by Lisa Coleman.*

Students had indeed arrived at the "happy hunting grounds," metaphorically speaking—the northeastern end of the ringed enclosure. Here, we were going to dig in our hunt for the "lost" sixth ring.[37]

"Y'all pick out a test pit where you want to work, and don't worry, they're all in the shade. No more'n three people to a pit, but remember to take turns digging and screening and filling out level reports. Call me or Carl when it's time to do the profiles. Go ahead and string off your pit. Tapes and line levels are in the toolbox. Remember stakes with coordinates and elevations written on them are the datum stakes, so run the line-level string from them. When you're finished, come back over here. I want to say a few words."[38]

From then on, walking the log became the closest thing we had to an initiation rite for university students on officially entering Poverty Point's sacred grounds for pilgrimages and field schools. It was reserved for those times when a lot of the participants were meeting for the first time, and, in the case of field schools, when acquaintances or total strangers from different universities were brought together one day and were expected to live and work together seamlessly for the coming weeks. Walking the log was our prescription for commonweal, for creating one big, happy family and lasting memories.

It's been years since anyone walked the log, but last time I checked, that old slippery foot log was still there, spanning the Harlin chasm, awaiting a new generation of log walkers.

High Ho, Tippy Toe
Just a-walking the log.

3

LOCUST STORIES

Long ago, Clarence Webb proposed that a class of polished-stone zoomorphic beads from Poverty Point and older sites resembled locusts.[39] Although the beads were highly stylized, the common denominator was a pair of raised discs or engraved circles on opposite sides of the midbody, which Webb likened to the auditory membranes of locusts. If there's not something attention-getting or mystical in having a bug so little make a noise so loud, a person either would have to be deaf or work in a planing mill.

Since Webb's pronouncement half a century ago, additional discoveries have revealed that zoomorphs exhibiting the disc/circle motif include birds, mammals and chimeras.[40] If we really knew what animals or ideas were intended, it is likely that they, too, would be represented in the folklore of animistic tribal peoples, but whether correctly identified or not, it is the locust that makes the incidents I recount below memorable. And its life cycle was the source of Native fascination—a thirteen-year metamorphosis from underground-dwelling grubworm to winged adult, which only lives a month—but, oh, what a month, one solely devoted to singing and mating.

It's not hard to envision the "connection" to the Choctaw creation story, in which grasshoppers (locusts) emerged from the top of an earthen mound along with the first humans (see the "Choctaw Creation"). It's easy to see the "connection" to Choctaw pneumatology, in which death released a person's two inner shadows, *shilup* and *shilombish*, leaving behind an empty shell (nymph exoskeleton).[41] The Koasati picked "roasting ears" (green corn) and snap beans when they heard the cicadas sing.[42]

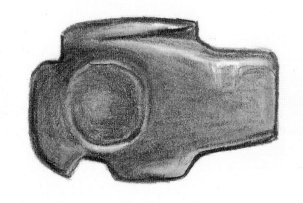

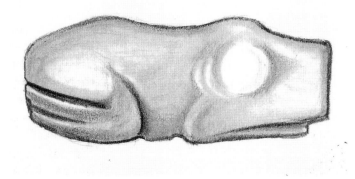

Locust beads
from Poverty
Point. *Drawn by
Jon Gibson.*

CHOCTAW CREATION

Choctaw traditionalists believed that the first people emerged from a cave
that opened in the top of an earthen mound and, after drying out, scattered
throughout the South, becoming the several Muskogean nations.[43] This
central narrative metaphorically references the human birth process and the
locust life cycle, as depicted in the following account.

> *Soon after the earth (yahne) was made, men and grasshoppers came to
> the surface through a long passageway that led from a large cavern in the
> interior of the Earth to the summit of a high hill, Nane' chaha. There,
> deep down in the Earth, in the great cavern, man and grasshoppers had
> been created by Aba, the Great Spirit, having been formed of yellow clay.*[44]

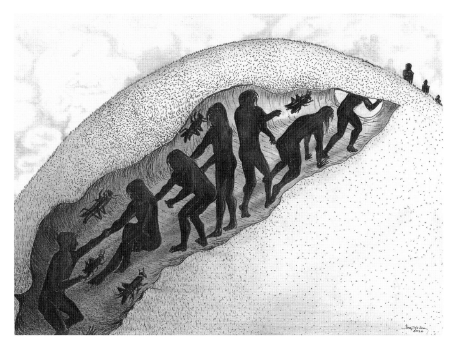

The Choctaw creation story. Made of clay by the Great Spirit, first people and grasshoppers came into the world from a cave that opened in the summit of a sacred mound, *Nanih Waiya. Drawn by Jon Gibson.*

To some mound-building peoples, mounds were known as "Navels of the Earth," figurative wombs.[45] To carry the allegory further, all one has to do is envision Poverty Point's principal mound-defined alignment as the umbilical cord of human birth, the tie to the ancestors and the pathway to the "Land of the Ghosts."[46]

As with all things, there is alterity, and the symbolism I see here will be another's bunkum. But that really doesn't matter because it's all about what you believe at the moment anyway. It has nothing to do with existence or science or disagreement—never did.

SINGING LOCUSTS AND THE WAILING WALL TEST PIT

The pit crew referred to the unit they were digging as the Wailing Wall Pit. Located in woods on the third embankment in the northern sector of the ringed enclosure, the pit was one of the deepest we ever excavated at Poverty Point, reaching more than eleven feet down.

"Doc, come over here and listen. There's some kinda noise down here," Ty said, looking up at me from the bottom of the pit.

"Yep, I heard it, too," exclaimed Marc, who had just scampered out of the hole. "Sumpin' weird's going on in that hole."

"Come on out, Ty," I said, setting the ladder in the pit. "Let me get down there."

Halfway down, I heard the drone, the pitch rising and falling almost like a train passing in the distance, its lonesome whistle blowing. As I stepped off the last rung and onto the hard, wet floor of the pit, the sound enveloped me, almost like the surround sound of a stereo. There was no obvious cause, and it was unnerving. "Gracious sakes," I thought, "Haven't we had enough crazy goings-on already? Now, we got a test pit that's humming."

I touched the wall. It seemed to be vibrating. I pressed my ear to the wall; the hum appeared to be coming out of the dirt. OK, that was enough. I quickly climbed out of the pit, mystified. The drone from the locusts in the trees around us was even more oppressive than the strange emanation down in the pit. "Beats me," I said. "Let's get the line level and graph paper so we can get the profiles done, an' then, let's close this baby up."

Marc jumped back down in the pit and began trowel-shaving the walls. The pit was as deep as we needed to go anyway. I recognized this as soon as I stepped onto the red-and-green-gleyed clay on the pit's bottom. The clay was a substratum in the old natural landform.

Marc paused his troweling and cocked his head. "Guess what," he said. "The sound's stopped."

Now, that was odd. The locusts above also had a momentary respite in their chorus. Then, the singing in the trees resumed, a shrill crescendo building to epic proportions.

"Doc, the sound's back—louder'n ever," Marc exclaimed.

I understood then. The sound was coming from the locusts. The deep pit was acting like an echo chamber, absorbing the drone from the trees and lowering the pitch in the process. Nothing was going to come out of the vibrating walls. There was no earthquake or nearby seismic testing. The locust that lit on my T-shirt sleeve seemed to offer that assurance.

"The sound's just the locusts, boys," I semi-confidently asserted. "It's their singing. It gets remixed in the pit and rebounds off the walls."

Ty and Marc glanced at each other. I could tell they wanted to believe me.

THE LOCUST AND THE SACRED TREE

The night was black—so black that the glow from 'Houn's cigarette looked like it was circling around by itself. A handful of us were sitting at the picnic tables behind the dormitory, bending elbows and telling yarns. Most of the field school students had gone to the crystal mines at Hot Springs for the weekend, but we old hands stayed behind, unwilling to give up a single moment of Poverty Point time, not even for crystals.

"Darn mosquito," complained Greg. "Any spray left in that can?"

"Here, Greg," said 'Houn. "Try some of this stuff. It's got Deet in it and lasts longer."

'Houn lit another cigarette and coughed dryly. The flame from his Zippo momentarily lit up the dogwood branch drooping over the table.

"What's that?" Lisa asked. "Look, hanging off the leaf."

"'Houn, strike your lighter over here."

As the light flickered up into the branches, we could see locusts' shed skins stuck onto the bottom of nearly every leaf. The entire dogwood was covered. The scene reminded me of bats hanging in a cave. It was then that we realized how many of the red-eyed songsters it had taken to create the hum in the Wailing Wall Pit. The woods must be alive with these insects.

The sight evoked primal memories. We all momentarily shared the reverence tribal peoples felt for the locust—the emergence of broods, the month of song, bespoke an ancient natural cycle. Nature's magic, nature's ritual had been woven into the cultural fabric, humans' ritual. At that moment, we, too, would have harvested green corn at the song's onset, we would have carved locust fetishes in red jasper, we would have recited the creation story based on its birth cycle.[47] We were caught up in ancient mysteries.

We talked about these things. We were glad our dig coincided with their ancient regimen, but the mood had grown somber. Without the lighter's flame, the darkness was total. Although the stars, even the Milky Way, sparkled through the treetops overhead, you couldn't see your hand in front of your face. Something profound was about to happen—you could feel it in your bones. The locusts' song stopped abruptly, but the night air remained vibrant.

The tree remained hidden, despite being only a few steps away from where we sat. Countless people passed right by it and never noticed it. A chosen handful of us always visited the tree during our sojourns at Poverty Point. I even carried a sliver of it in the dove seat where I kept my trowels, tapes and

Sacred tree metamorphosis. *Drawn by Donna Trahan.*

line levels for luck. I don't know when the "sacred tree" appellation started, probably with Mitchell, but it somehow seemed appropriate for this unusual tree. You see, the tree had two trunks, the larger one was a white oak, the other, a dogwood. The graft had occurred so long ago, there was no seam at the joining.

The tree seemed to beckon. I picked up the Maglite and bade the others to follow. The flashlight beam illuminated the sacred tree as we moved through the dense mandrake undergrowth, deeper into the dogwood thicket. I flashed the light back on the ground.

"Y'all watch where you step," I implored. "Don't need to step on a cottonmouth."

I climbed over the familiar rotten log and waited for the others to catch up. When everyone had crossed the log, I shined the beam back on the tree. For a while, nobody noticed anything. Then somebody said, "Look, two trees have grown together. Finally, all recognized what they had been looking at. They awakened to another dimension, the hidden dimension of Poverty Point.

That's when we saw the birth. The locust slowly pushed its way through the slit in the back of its old nymph skin. There, on the underside of a dogwood leaf, it clung upside down to the hollow shell, while its ghostly pale body slowly turned a metallic green. We continued to watch, spellbound, as it climbed on top of the dogwood leaf nursery, fluttered its membranous wings and buzzed away into the darkness. A barred owl hooted nearby, announcing the birth.

There, on the dogwood half of the sacred tree, we had just watched the birth of a locust—not just any locust, mind you, but a Poverty Point locust. At that moment, we were quite sure we had witnessed the birth of *the* Poverty Point locust, the very same one that inspired the old ones' sacred carvings and gave rise to their origin story.

Everyone broke off a twig from the dogwood and stuck it in their pocket for luck.

THE LOCUST SONG AND THE *SHILOMBISH*

Twenty-six people gathered around 5599/5000, the test unit on the North Three embankment, where the official groundbreaking ceremony for the 1989 excavation season was about to take place. A hush fell over the group when I stepped up to the string-outlined test pit, shovel in hand. Everyone waited for me to say something important that would memorialize the occasion.

I paused. The moment was not yet right. There was whispering.

I waited for absolute silence, but silence never came. Instead, it was the humming, loud and shrill, rising and falling. The humming loosed long-dormant memories. For a split second, I found myself standing outside an old unpainted house on a hill above Castor Creek, staring at the black

Chula or *Shilombish* watches Gina and Doc excavate test pits, while Lisa plots a view of the earth oven on grid paper on Bertha Hale Knoll, Poverty Point. *Drawn by Donna Trahan.*

locust trees behind the chicken coop. It was my childhood home. The same humming used to come from those trees. "But how could trees hum?" I wondered.

Then I remembered my grandpa showing me the shed skin and the buzzing insect with the red eyes and explaining that the grubs we used for fish bait were really locust nymphs, which only came out of the ground every so often.

I understood. I was listening to the locust song.

The emotional moment passed. I had the undivided attention of the students. Then the time was right. Shovel in hand, I started to speak when I was interrupted by a shape coming toward us. It was a fox, the fox with yellow fur, the light-colored fox that many of us had begun to identify with the *shilombish* because of his appearance at especially propitious moments.

Everyone turned to look. The fox-form drew within a truck length of the knot of students before he veered away and, unhurriedly, vanished into the thick undergrowth in the Harlin Bayou bottom. Everyone was stunned.

No words came. None were necessary.

I threw a shovelful of dirt onto the screen and watched fixedly as it filtered through the quarter-inch mesh in a dozen little streams. Everyone stared at the shed locust skin that was left on the screen and understood that this excavation season would be one to remember.

It was named the Season of the Singing Locust.

4
FOX STORIES

One morning before K.B. shooed us out of her lab, Lorraine and I were cogitating about the failure to find human remains at Poverty Point in light of the large number of people who were believed to have lived there. We were discussing means for disposing of the dead that might not have left remains when she casually mentioned Choctaw burial customs, including their belief in the deceased's two spirits.[48] Her reminder about the *shilombish*, the spirit that remained on earth in the form of an owl or a fox, caught my attention immediately. Hooting owls lulled us to sleep every night, and foxes often played in Poverty Point's plaza, and we presumed many people had died here.

The old Choctaw people, like other Muskogean tribes, believed in a dual afterlife; *Shilup i Yokni*, the Land of Ghosts, and *Atuklant Illi*, (the Land of) the Second Death, are reminiscent of Christians' Heaven and Hell.[49] The Land of Ghosts was a place of perpetual sunlight, warmth, happiness, health and plenty, and the Land of Second Death was a place of everlasting misery, reserved for murderers. According to Albert Wright, going to one place or the other did not depend on being good or bad or on believing in a supreme being, but—except for murderers—it was reliant on being able, perchance, to find the right path. Even bad people could enter the Land of Ghosts if they happened to be lucky enough to find the right way.

The old people believed that everyone had two souls, or shadows.[50] The *shilup*, or inside shadow (ghost), always accompanies the person and, on their death, goes to the Land of Ghosts. The *shilombish*, or outside shadow, remains on earth and:

> [W]*anders about its former habitation, and often, especially at night, by its pitiful moans, so to affrighten its surviving friends, as to make them forsake the spot, and seek another abode. It is also supposed frequently to assume the form of a fox, or owl; and, by barking like the one, and screeching like the other at night causes great consternation, for the cry is ominous of ill.*[51]

The fox was *chula* to the Choctaw or, in spirit form, he was *shilombish*, the outside shadow. To us at Poverty Point, he was both. Some people saw him leading Walker hounds on spirited chases around the mounds and across the rings. Some spied him sitting near the Great Mound watching and smiling, ears erect, listening. A select few even witnessed the vixen escorting her kits on locust-chasing expeditions across the grassy tops of the rings near her den in the Dunbar Ravine. Still others never saw the fox. Seeing it came to be regarded as a privilege and inspired fascination—even awe. Stories of sightings were told and retold at the commons area in the dorm and at the nightly summit meetings on Mound B, wherever students gathered—even at Sonny's.[52]

Varied *Shilombish* guises, an antlered headdress, striped face mask, cloaked body dance fan and sweeping arms-wings. *Drawn by Jon Gibson.*

Shilombish attends a groundbreaking during the locust song on the north three embankment. *Drawn by Donna Trahan.*

Unlike the Choctaw *shilombish*, *seeing* the yellow-furred Poverty Point spirit-fox was not considered scary or unlucky—just the opposite. The yellow-furred fox always seemed to bring good fortune if one but recognized the meaning.

The fox was not only a Choctaw character. Poverty Point's ancients also knew this *chula*, this *shilombish*. They engraved likenesses of its alter-egos on magnetite plummets and slate gorgets. They gave it human qualities, an antlered headdress, a face mask, a cloaked-body dance fan and sweeping arms-wings—representations we collectively call the fox-man.[53] The ancients recognized the duality of the fox, and they could tell the difference between *chula* and *shilombish*.

Shilombish and the Crystal Drill

What makes the *shilombish* story intriguing is a strange series of "coincidences" that transpired during the 1988 field season. This was our first field season without Mitchell, the curator of the commemorative area and longtime friend, as he had suffered a fatal heart attack at Poverty Point the year before.[54]

Poverty Point was Mitchell's place. He was born and raised practically within sight of the Great Mound, perhaps, as some thought, as one of the ancients reincarnated. Mitchell did seem to possess the ancient wisdom—to know things others didn't, to "see" things others couldn't. This combined with his probing, analytical mind and his easy-going, folksy character, earned him the reputation of seer, a modern-day shaman, especially with the scores of young people who worked with him at Poverty Point and on various cultural resource projects across the South. Prophetically, long before he died, people had begun to associate Mitchell with the fox, the fox-man.[55] An underground "society" even grew up around him.

Now, with all the fox sightings and paw prints, more than one eyebrow was raised at the suggestion that Mitchell was still here, watching, listening, marking places of interest. I heard these stories and will admit to looking for meaning in them—some answer, some foretelling, some shortcut to conventional understanding. I had yet to see the fox this season but did find fresh tracks in the back dirt around our excavation units, notably the "Five-Legged Spider" Pit mentioned in the epigraph.

The fox-marked pit did raise expectations about what would be found there. Pit crews working there all became instant Indiana Joneses, searching for the Lost Ark or the Holy Grail. Deeper and deeper they dug, but they found nothing out of the ordinary—no coveted owl pendant, no locust bead, not even a gray flint Motley point, just more PPOs.

Fox tracks single out the crystal drill pit. *Drawn by Jon Gibson.*

Just as digging was starting to become routine, Brooks stood up and summoned, "Hey, Doc, you might better come over here and look at this." He held up a slender quartz crystal to the sunlight. Colors of the rainbow danced through a narrow band around its middle. The crystal had been bruised by heavy rotation. It was a drill bit.

"Well," said Brooks, "at least it ain't another PPO."

This was certainly not the golden treasure Hollywood would have scripted, and it was not particularly noteworthy in its own right, except for the historical novelty of being the first of its kind to be discovered at Poverty Point. Then, Brooks realized what he was holding. "It's a crystal drill like Doctor Jay was talking about last night, idden't it?"

"Looks like it," I acknowledged. "The spider and the fox both marked the spot."

The irony of the discovery was immediately recognized by three dozen spectators. Jay had previously identified identical crystal drills at the Slate site and other Poverty Point components in the Yazoo Basin and had just finished writing a paper announcing them.[56] They were the subject of his lecture at the dorm the night before.

Quartz crystals had been found at Poverty Point, but never before had a crystal drill been recognized. Now, standing next to the discovery pit at the exact moment of its unearthing was the archaeologist who first recognized them. Coincidence, you say? You might want to check the odds.

The crystal drill, the archaeologist who first realized what they were, the discovery site marked by the wise old spider and the wily fox and three dozen witnesses joined in space-time and spirit. The gentle breeze that caressed the assembly carried away any lingering doubt as to whether the fox-form that marked the spot was *chula* or *shilombish*.

As if to memorialize the occasion, there was a shout from an adjacent pit. "I keep telling y'all, duplication's good, and it's got rainbow colors in the middle, too."

"Let's see—two crystal drills discovered within minutes of each other, along with the crystal man himself as witness—so, Doctor Jay, what do you have to say about all this?"

"Another paper shot to hell."[57]

SHILOMBISH AND SAMPLING, PART 1

I pulled my Chevy four-by-four into the parking space at the lab. Dennis was waiting on the porch, chewing on his Swisher Sweet. "You made good time."

"Yeah, I took the shortcut at Leland and bypassed that one-lane stretch at Sicily Island."

"Let's take the park's pickup," said Dennis. "Throw your stuff in the back end. My seat's kinda full."

"We can use my truck. At least, there's room to sit."

"Nawh, climb in. I got the maps in here an' flagging tape, too."

We rolled down the windows and slowly drove along the narrow strip of asphalt across the concentric rings, bent on flagging the spots where I wanted to dig. We had planned to set flags back in March, during pilgrimage, but heavy rain forced us to stay indoors, close to the cooler.

Choosing dig areas was really a simple matter: pick out landscape irregularities in order to tell whether they were natural or man-made. Since we aspired to dig them all, there was no need for a sampling plan in any of its statistical iterations.[58] Eventually, however, our work for the upcoming season did entail adopting a highly unusual sampling procedure.

As we approached the Great Mound, the faint smell of wild onions and dampness from the flooded aisle drifted through the open windows. Poverty Point's creatures began coming out to greet us. An armadillo waddled nonchalantly out of the tree line, followed by a fox squirrel that scampered up the mound slope and jumped onto the nearest red oak, where it stopped and fussed at us, tail jerking. The jittery squirrel was immediately shadowed by a raccoon, which ambled stiff-leggedly over to a stunted dogwood and climbed up to the first fork. Dennis stopped the truck, and we walked toward the dogwood. "Where'd that 'coon go," he asked? "I didn't see him get out of the tree."

"Me neither."

Strange. The tree was only as tall as a basketball goal and was solid as a phone pole. Mystified, we trudged back to the pickup. I asked, "Have you seen the fox?"

"Not lately," he replied.

We scrambled back into the truck and headed out into sunlit the Mound B field. Leaving the cool, dark woods, I had a strong feeling that we were about to see the fox. I cleaned off the midden on Dennis's dashboard to provide an uncluttered view. We rounded Mound B, and suddenly, there he was. The fox trotted along the crest of the Northwest Six embankment, a section of the outer ring of the ringed enclosure. Although a line of trees was only a bound away, he was out in the open, in plain sight. Unhurried by the approaching pickup, he continued to trot along the embankment, crossed the narrow road and, without ever glancing our way, vanished into the thick undergrowth in the Harlin Bayou bottom. I noticed how tawny his coat seemed.

I bade Dennis to stop the truck, grabbed a roll of flagging tape, strode over to a clump of switch cane where the fox disappeared and tied ribbons on three of the tallest canes. Here, on this fox-marked spot, we would dig—on this spot we called Fox Run.

I didn't look for the *shilombish* in the bottom. I knew he was there, and I knew he was watching.

Hiding in this story is one of the most ingenious sampling procedures ever used to select excavation units. It is called: the "let the fox pick them" sampling strategy.

SHILOMBISH AND SAMPLING, PART 2

I glanced at the digital clock glued on my truck dash; it was almost 9:30 a.m. Erin and I were returning from setting up our charge account at the Bestway Grocery store in Epps. Erin's my daughter. She was taking my field school for the credit, although, when she was little, she did like to "hunt arrowheads" with her dad.

"Daddy, Erin exclaimed excitedly, "there's the fox!" Erin had heard fox stories before.

He was sitting out in the open near the black walnut tree on the Northwest One embankment near where another university had dug several years previously, almost as if he was waiting for us. We slowed and watched while he bounded down the back side of Northwest One, crossed the narrow park road atop Northwest Two and vanished into the woods along Harlin Bayou, his golden-brown coat shining in the sun. I swung the pickup off the state highway and onto the park road, stopping where he entered the woods. We tied flagging to the limb of a fallen tree. This would be another excavation site. The fox had chosen it.

The next day, we found a yellow jacket nest in the roots of the fallen tree where I tied the flagging and discovered that the fox's path followed the main north–south baseline of the permanent grid control system we had established years before. "Search for the Lost Sixth Ridge" was the Indiana Jones–like title I concocted for our current field work and T-shirt logo. I was not surprised at all when we found that the fox's path headed straight for where the "lost ridge" should have been.

The sampling strategy was working again.

SEARCH FOR THE LOST SIXTH RIDGE

When I found out that Francis had arranged for Louisiana Public Broadcasting to film our dig, I was determined to christen the field season with a catchy title that would not be outdone by Hollywood's recent films, Spielberg's *Raiders of the Lost Ark* and Auel's *Clan of the Cave Bear*. "Search for the Lost Sixth Ridge" was my final bow to cinematic labeling, but the title was dead-on, too. We really were going to look for evidence that the sixth, or outer, ring had once encircled the entire enclosure. There was no visible sign of a sixth ring in the northern sector that day.

We faced two possibilities for its absence: it was either never built or had been destroyed. Since all other aisle-separated compartments in the enclosure bore the full complement of six rings, we suspected it had been erased by erosion from Harlin Bayou, but we wanted to find proof. The bayou was the suspected culprit because it directly impinged onto the outermost northern ring. Harlin was nothing more than a deep, headward-cutting ravine that had been activated by postconstruction rerouted runoff. Thus, its mischief, we reasoned, took place because of ring building.

To prove or disprove our supposition, 'Houn, Marvin (also known as Doctor J., not Doctor Jay) and I laboriously ran grid out to two spots along the high bank of the bayou, which stuck out into the chasm. These little projections were about as far away from the fifth ring as you could get without falling down the steep bank. Here, we staked off two test units. Like true scientists, we surmised that if basket-loaded evidence for a sixth ring still existed, back here is where it would be found. The next day, with renewed vigor and only dull headaches, we hand pulled a slew of solid cores with a tube sampler and found no basket-loading.

"Whatcha think, Doctor J.?"

"Well, Doctor G., sure looks like natural soil to me."

The woods seemed a bit darker and drearier the following morning as the field crew gathered around the test pits along the bayou bank. Putting on a cheery face, I explained why we had chosen to put the test pits where we had.

"Doc, you want us to go get the shovels and screens?"

"Nawh, hold on a second. Let me tell y'all why we decided to dig here, and then you can tell me what you think," I said, propping on the soil probe.

"Several years back, J.E. Chance & Associates mapped Poverty Point for us. One small-scale map was based on an aerial flyover and had half-meter contours, and the other map was engineered by professional surveyors using a total station, but it only encompassed the southwestern section of the rings, not the whole enclosure. Contours were drawn at ten-centimeter intervals. Now, get this, and this is important," I continued. "When we measured distances between midlines of the southwestern rings, we found they were uniformly spaced, forty-three meters apart, except for the space between ring one and ring two, which was sixty meters across. Now, here, we put these two test pits twenty-two and twenty-five meters from where the center of ring five was judged to be, and that's more'n half the distance between ring crests everywhere else. So, if the spacing is the same everywhere, what do you think all this means?" I asked.

"Well," Charlotte answered quickly, "if y'all didn't hit basket-loading, then it has to mean that the spacing between rings is not the same everywhere or else the Indians didn't build a sixth ring back here."

"Right, that's what it looks like."

"Shoot," exclaimed Albert. "So, if's there's no ring back here, where we gonna dig now?"

That posed no problem. We had plenty of other places earmarked in our long-term effort to identify the built part of the landscape, Poverty Point's culture-scape. The remainder of our days at Poverty Point passed normally, unless you count a humming test pit, a metamorphizing sacred locust and fox sightings as being abnormal. Take my word for it, at Poverty Point, such incidents are the norm, not the exception.

Still, I couldn't get the lost sixth ring out of my head. Everything else about the earthwork was so symmetrical. Why would builders have left off the northeastern end of the outer ring? The ring was present everywhere else. It just didn't make sense.

Near the dig's end, I yielded to temptation and prevailed on Thurman, my soil scientist partner, to bring his core truck to the far northeastern end of the enclosure, near the mouth of Harlin Bayou, and pull a deep core with the hydraulic Bull sampler. With Debbie and Joan, visiting friends from the state parks office, guiding the truck and with me hanging on the rear bumper, trying to prevent, I hoped, the truck from overturning, Thurman coaxed the truck between trees and rills until he finally maneuvered it into a level position where he could take the core. Unfortunately, the core only showed a natural soil profile—no basket loading here either.

It was beginning to look like the builders hadn't finished the northeastern end of outer ring after all. Disappointed, I climbed down onto a large section of the bank that had slumped downslope and started throwing acorns at tail-slapping garfish in the bayou below. But the last projectile I picked up was not an acorn but a small PPO fragment.

"Hey, Thurman, guess what? We got some PPOs down here and some dark soil."

"Hang on, Jon, let me get the hand probe."

Thurman slid down the bank and punched a core in the slump block and then several more. With the end of a chair spindle, he extruded the solid cylinder of soil out of the tube sampler and feathered the dirt between his fingers, not giving up a thing until finally, "Well," he drawled, "it's got a mixture of textures an' colors, an' it's got some basal clays in it, too. Ya know, Jon, this stuff looks like basket loading to me."

Debbie, Joan and I climbed into the bed of Thurman's truck for the ride out of the deep woods and into the sunlight of the plaza. The locusts were singing loudly. I recalled the path the fox form had followed earlier in the season, the path that led straight toward the lost ring.

With the lost ring found and my lost faith restored, I told the fox story to Debbie and Joan.

I should have known better than to question the existence of the sixth ring in the first place. The ancient builders certainly hadn't forgotten it, but the *shilombish* had to show us where to look.

The Playful Fox

John Calhoun relates a story about the antics of the fox following the 1985 field school.

> *Each night,* [Dennis] *would spend two or three hours sitting alone in the carport, carving a hardwood atlatl and working an intricate Poverty Point design—the fox-man, a stylized human/fox pattern portrayed on magnetite plummets—from the tip to the handle. Within a week after Mitchell had been laid to rest, Dennis was joined in his late-night vigil. As he worked the wood, he suddenly had the feeling of another presence. When he looked up from the work, he saw, sitting just at the edge of the light, ears erect and staring intently at him, an adult red fox. As Dennis stared, the animal cocked its head to one side, rose and quietly disappeared into the darkness.*
>
> *Dennis was not quite as surprised the following night, or the night after that, and each night, the fox seemed more at ease, moving closer, and staying longer. Within two weeks, the animal would curl up on the pavement not ten feet in front of Dennis's chair and seemingly listen as Dennis spent his two hours carving and talking.*

A fox-man totem carved by Dennis LaBatt in memory of the playful fox. *Drawn by Jon Gibson.*

At the onset, Dennis had been leerier than the fox. It was a mature adult male and healthy. Its behavior was atypical but not rabid. Or maybe not atypical for Poverty Point. One night, at the time he was usually on the carport, Dennis was talking with Jon Gibson on the telephone, and there was a scratching at the window. Dennis pulled back the curtain, and in the light, pressed against the glass pane was the muzzle and right front paw of the fox.

The parking lot of the dormitory adjacent to Dennis's house had recently been paved, and one morning, he, his wife and two small girls were playing kickball on the fresh surface, when, out of the tree line, the fox approached and sat in the open field in front of the dorm, watching. After a few minutes, it moved to the edge of the pavement and sat still. Soon, it began running back and forth along the grass next to the pavement with the girls, in much the same way a pet dog would romp with children. Dennis became concerned and shouted the fox away. He retreated to his first position and watched the rest of the game, and when they finished playing and returned to the houses, he slipped into the woods.[59]

I remember Dennis's call and the incredulousness in his voice. We talked for several minutes with the fox eavesdropping, and never once did the fox break eye contact. Only when we hung up did the fox fade into the night from where he came. The incident made such an impression on us both that Dennis carved a dogwood branch in his image, and thereafter, whenever I was at Poverty Point, I would discreetly erect the carved fox-man totem in a hidden location for the duration.

The Invisible Fox

We finished boxing all the artifacts and paperwork and cleaning the tools. Bright and early the next day, we would load the pickups and say our goodbyes to Poverty Point—another excavation season completed, a new family created, our respects paid to the old ones.

At sunset, the remaining skeleton crew—the Old Guard, as they called themselves—piled into the bed of Lisa's orange Nissan pickup for one last circuit of the site. The brilliant red sun slid behind the tree line, sending daggers of light through the branches and bathing the Nissan with a warm glow. The passengers grew quiet, not wanting to frighten away any of Poverty Point's creatures that might be awaiting our farewell lap. The faces peering into the darkening woods revealed the anticipation of seeing the fox. We had not seen him since the morning of opening day, and afternoon chatter was all about taking a fox-watch walkabout after work.

We had not gone very far, when, suddenly, there he was, out in the open, near the Causeway. Lisa stopped the truck, and we all stared silently, grateful for the privilege of being allowed to bid the fox adieu.

He lay perfectly still, ears erect, hind legs spread-eagle, cooling his belly on the newly fallen dew. He stared back at us, fox eyes narrowed to slits.

Lisa started the truck and turned off the narrow asphalt road toward him. That was too much. We lost sight of him as he bounded into the trees along the Causeway, headed toward the mound we call Ballcourt Mound.[60]

Lisa pulled back onto the road and started around the Great Mound, entering the lengthening shadows. We felt content. The fox had attended our opening ceremony, and on our last official day of field work, the day before we were to leave Poverty Point, the fox had come to bid us farewell.

"'Til we meet again, old friend," said 'Houn.

Everyone was smiling, and quiet natter resumed. As we rounded the Great Mound, a raccoon ambled stiff-leggedly across the road, heading for the same little dogwood tree where Dennis and I had seen a similar event play out weeks before. "This can't be happening again," I thought. "It's déjà vu all over again," Yogi's words popped into my head. That's when I realized that the fox was not done with us yet.

We drove out into the shadows of Mound B field. A single ray of light illuminated a lone fox standing at the edge of the woods. "Look, everybody," I exclaimed. "There, next to the tree-line."

Nobody saw him—strange, as he was standing there in plain sight, fur shining like being bathed in a spotlight. But wait—this couldn't be the same fox we had seen moments before. That fox had run off in the opposite direction, toward Ballcourt Mound, and there would not have been enough time for him to have circled back. No, this had to be another fox. Then it dawned on me. This was, indeed, a different fox, an invisible fox. He had yellow fur, and he was smiling broadly. "Yep," I said and nodded, as Mitchell and I always did on leaving each other's company. Then he faded into the shadows and was gone.

VISION OF THE FOX-MAN

The dream was so real that I can remember asking myself if it was all really happening or if it was a dream. When I woke up, I knew the answer. I usually don't remember dreams, much less anything about their manifest content, so I figured my clear recall of this dream was due to the Poverty Point effect. But apparently, even that only reaches so deep, else the dream's latent content would have been revealed, too.

Let me start from the dream's beginning.

Wade showed up at the dorm just past sunset one afternoon and told me there was someone up at the lab who wanted to see me. He said that Mitchell had told him to tell me to bring some little thing I considered lucky but wasn't worth anything. It was a strange request, I thought, and I began to wonder what Mitchell was up to. I went inside, put on my boots, pulled my lucky frog-colored Hula Popper out of my tackle box and walked out into the parking lot, where Wade was waiting in the "Blue Goose." We headed toward the lab.

I noticed Wade was unusually quiet, but when he passed the entrance gate to the lab, I knew something was going on. Nobody was waiting to see me. I asked him where we were going, but all he would say was that it was just down the road a little. Sure enough, just outside the park's southern fence, he turned onto the gas field road that ran back toward the crater, where a drilling rig had been engulfed by an erupting gas pocket years before, leaving a deep, now-willow-hidden pond inhabited by bullfrogs and goggle-eye.

When we got close to the crater, Wade stopped the Blue Goose and switched off the headlights. I could barely make out the road ahead. I asked him why he had stopped, and he said the fox-man told him to. The fox-man?

We got out of the truck, and Wade pulled out an old blowing horn from under his seat. It was the same turkey feather–adorned blowing horn that I had seen hanging in Mitchell's gun cabinet. He handed it to me and told me to blow it, or they wouldn't invite us in. Who were they? Invite us where? What did Mitchell's blowing horn have to do with any of this? None of this was making any sense, but it was beginning to look like Mitchell was involved.

Vision of the white-faced man conducting a ritual. *Drawn by Jon Gibson.*

Still perplexed, I put the horn to my pursed lips and blew, but the result sounded more like a squeaky clarinet than the clarion call of a hunting bugle. I handed the horn back to Wade, and he blasted out three long, mournful wails, loud and clear. That worked because, immediately, a huge bonfire lit up the clearing ahead, and three blasts from a blowing horn answered Wade's call. Wade, who seemed to have been through a similar surreal happening before, said that was the signal for us to join the ceremony. "Whoa, wait a minute," I thought. "What ceremony? Who said anything about a ceremony?"

Oh, I had heard rumors before, but I thought they were just that—rumors. But here I was dreaming about animated rumors in technicolor, complete with biblical-style trumpet blasts.

In the clearing, I could see three backlit silhouettes standing by the leaping fire. I grew even more apprehensive until I saw that two of the three fire-lit faces were those of 'Houn and Burney. The third figure I didn't recognize because his face was painted white, and he wore a fox skin pulled over his head and a deerskin cape around his shoulders. Behind him stood a tall bamboo pole with a crown of deer horns and all manner of objects dangling from it. The white-faced guy was holding a turkey-feather fan in one hand and gourd rattle in the other. Bands of jingle bells were tied below his knees, and he wore Taos-style moccasins. He was saying a bunch of stuff, most of which I barely heard, but I recognized the voice. It was Mitchell's.

I vaguely remember him saying that if you agree with these principles, stay where you are, and if not, you can leave now. Mitchell paused. We all looked at each other, but nobody left. He had us go through some symbolic gyrations, including tying our lucky items to the bamboo totem pole, and then he proclaimed us to be "card-carrying" members of some secret group. He told us to remember the symbol he had drawn in the dirt and to put the token he had given us in a safe place.

I was halfway back to the Blue Goose when I woke up, or so I thought, still unsure about what had just happened. Wade was leaning against the fender. "I tol' you somebody wanted to see you, jus' didn't say it was the fox-man himself. He said you'd figure it out quick enough."

When I finally awoke from the dream the next morning, I assumed I had been having a dream within a dream. Still, I wondered why my tackle box was open. It was several weeks later before I figured out why.

Field school had ended, and I was bass fishing in Routh Creek, near where it empties into Catahoula Lake. My shallow-running spinner bait caught an underwater snag and broke off. Wishing to avoid a repeat performance in the brush-filled creek, I reached for a weedless top-water lure—my lucky frog-colored Hula Popper. Strange, it was not in the tackle box. Where could it be? It was then that I remembered where I had tied it.

5
HUMAN INTEREST STORIES

Sometimes, events at Poverty Point take on an air of mystery because they can't be easily explained or else require explanations stranger than the incident itself. And then there are those events attributed to encounters with otherworldly beings or refugees from lost continents or interactions with nature's agents.

THE HOLLOW TREE DRUM

Once, long ago, a field school crew digging on the third embankment in the upper west compartment of the ringed enclosure noticed a faint arrhythmic thumping, almost like a drum beating occasionally in the distance. Some of the braver jocks, worried that something nefarious might be trying to scare the girls, set out to find the source of concern.

Their search revealed nothing.

The next day, the sound returned but not as often or as loud.

Everyone seemed to have grown accustomed to the inexplicable noise, or maybe they had begun to accept it as just another Poverty Point oddity. Then, the following day, one of the mapping team members was holding the stadia rod next to a small blackgum tree, when she shouted that she had located the noise, and it was coming from a tree. The mapping team hurried to the tree but heard nothing. Then the breeze picked up, and so did the sound, softly at first, *whump, whump,* then louder, *WHUMP, WHUMP,* then silence. When the breeze stirred, the tree throbbed—the harder the wind, the louder the sound.

Turns out, the tree was, indeed, the source of the drumming. As a sapling, the tree had two trunks, but one had withered and died, leaving a deep cavity where the dead fork decayed. It was filled with dark stump water and rimmed with resurrection fern. Every time a breath of wind dipped into the cavity, the water shimmered, and the thumping began.

Relief and disappointment registered on the faces of the mapping team— relief that the mysterious noise had been identified, disappointment that it was not a drumbeat echoing across the millennia.

But take note, Cushman observed:

> *The ancient Choctaw were as susceptible to all the pleasing emotions produced by the sweet concords of sound as any people, yet their musical genius, in, the invention of musical instruments, never extended beyond that of a cane flute and a small drum, which was constructed of a section cut from a small hollow tree over which was stretched a fresh deer skin, cleansed of the hair, which became very tight when dried; and when struck by a stick, made a dull sound…could still be heard at considerable distance; and though uncouth in appearance and inharmonious in tone…still "its" voice was considered an indispensable adjunct as an accompaniment to all their national and religious ceremonies.*[61]

Had Poverty Point's hollow tree drum taken root from ancient tree drums used on the spot thirty centuries before? Who can say it hadn't? Certainly not those of us who heard it beating on a moonlit night three decades ago.

Man Who Listens to Birds

Choctaw people have been coming to Poverty Point for many years. They display their crafts and conduct tribal events, but deep down, they choose to come to Poverty Point in keeping with an essential Nativeness that bonds Native peoples everywhere, past and present. It was in this latter vein that Angry Woman appeared.

Angry Woman had been to Poverty Point before. She was outspoken. She insisted that museum artifacts should not be exhibited but returned to Native peoples, their rightful owners. She complained about the trash left around the picnic tables and cigarette butts discarded on the parking lot. Her stares unnerved the staff. There were rumors about her being a card-carrying member of the once-radical American Indian Movement (AIM), as well as a *Hehyoka*, or a contrary, a person given to behavior outside the norms. But her behavior was not abnormal. It was normal for political advocacy. Still, she was part of the Choctaw delegation who had been officially granted use of the park facilities, including overnight accommodations in the dorm.

As part of the Poverty Point experience, the delegates were given a guided tour of the ancient earthworks. They met Dennis next morning and boarded the tram, Angry Woman among them. Dennis later told us that he knew the tour was going to be interesting before the tram had even made its first stop. It seems that one rider found the seats uncomfortably hot, the acoustics poor and viewing unremarkable. "Where are the ridges you said the old ones built? I don't see anything but clover."

"Yes, ma'am," Dennis replied. "We planted the clover to make the ridges stand out; they're only about three or four feet high out here where farmers used to plow. They're taller in the trees."

As the tram approached its first stop on the interior southwestern ring, Dennis's attention was drawn to the raucous cawing of a crow, and by the time it made the second stop at the steps leading up the "wing" of the Great Mound, the lone crow had been joined by several of her brothers. Their loud incessant cawing continued while the delegation climbed to the top of the Great Mound, during Dennis's spiel on the summit and on the return descent to the tram. People were starting to take notice.

The birds continued to join the others, and by the third stop at Mound B— the mound where mound building began at Poverty Point—their numbers had turned a boisterous septet into a gaggle rivaling Alfred Hitchcock's 1960s movie *The Birds*. Then everyone was watching the crows, wondering why they were following the tram. Dennis told the passengers not to worry, the crows were only testing him to make sure he told Poverty Point's story correctly.

That brought out mummering.

You see, the old Choctaw people regarded the crow as a bird of "evil omen," a harbinger of sinister events and a bearer of bad luck. In the story of the great flood, the crow ignored Good Man's plea to find dry land, where he could land his life raft.[62] Yet, like many legendary animals, the crow manifested a dual personality—it was the crow who brought maize to the people, thus providing the Choctaw and their ancestors with their staple food for a millennium.[63] So, which persona was shadowing the tram?

Dennis revved up the tram and proceeded to the next-to-last stop on the third ring in the northwestern part of the enclosure, the spot where we had excavated the Robert Parrish Test Pit. There, the birds began to quiet and disperse, and at the final stop at Dunbar Mound, the earth-covered stomp ground in the plaza, the last remaining crow swooped low over the watchful spectators and silently winged across the bayou.

"Musta got everything right, huh?" Dennis grinned.

"Those crows had us worried for a while," came a voice from the rear of the tram. "But a man who listens to birds is one straight arrow."

Dennis returned the group to the boarding area in the museum parking lot, and riders began disembarking, shaking his hand and thanking him for the informative tour. One person was noticeably missing from the grateful group, and Dennis saw her heading toward the picnic table beside the old laboratory. Dennis said it was then that an elderly gentleman came up to him and told him it would be good if he would go talk to her; he said she comes from good people and has a good heart. She gets lots of legal stuff done for the tribe.

She was sitting by herself, eating a sandwich, when Dennis approached. "May I sit?" Dennis asked, pulling out his package of jerky. "Hope you enjoyed the tour. Kinda warm today though."

"Glad you listen to the crows," she said. "They're wise and always tell the truth."

"Oh, yes, ma'am, I listen to all the totem animals. They keep you honest, teach you how to be respectful."

"Looks like Poverty Point's in good hands, Dennis."

"Well, thank you, miss, uuh."

"It's Crow, yeah, like the bird."

Crow and Dennis remain friends to this day.

ONION RINGS

Some of the most interesting discoveries at Poverty Point have not come by way of the Marshalltown but through remote sensing techniques such as aerial photography, multispectral imagery, ground-penetrating radar, magnetometry, electromagnetic conductivity and Mr. Joseph's purified water (see "Poverty Point and the New Atlantis, Part 1"). Ford discovered Poverty Point's concentric rings on a 1938 black-and-white aerial photograph taken from a high-flying airplane.[64]

Hargrave and Clay detected the remains of two dozen buried woodhenges by measuring magnetic field gradients with a sled-mounted gradiometer

Left: The Poverty Point discovery photograph, a 1938 aerial view of Poverty Point earthworks taken by the U.S. Army Engineers District in Vicksburg. *Courtesy of Shelia Lewis.*

Below: A printout of ground-penetrating radar imagery, showing natural soil and a buried hubcap. *Courtesy of James Doolittle (U.S. Soil Conservation Service).*

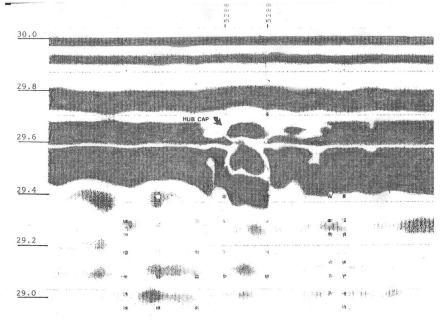

towed along the ground.[65] The imagery clearly showed circles of vacated post molds hidden beneath a waist-deep blanket of dirt. In another instance, a buried 1971 Chevrolet hubcap was detected with a ground-penetrating radar unit pulled behind a four-wheel-drive pickup.[66]

It was beginning to look like remote sensing might be the golden key to unlocking Poverty Point's deepest secrets, and what's more, it would not take an army of excavators to uncover them, only a computer screen and a geek. So, when word got out about NASA's thematic mapper simulator (TMS) and thermal infrared multispectral simulator (TIMS) technologies, excitement was as high as a punt returner waiting for the ball to come out of the stadium lights or a feature twirler awaiting halftime.

The science behind these technologies is for physicists and engineers, but their imaged data are like looking at frozen colorized frames of *The Waltons* or *Happy Days* reruns. Basically, these systems scan, sort and map differences in thermal radiation given off by various components on the earth's surface; vegetation, water, rock and soil all have distinctive heat signatures, and the instrumentation is so sensitive that it can detect differences well beyond what can be seen by the naked eye or optical cameras. Scans depict seven separate heat ranges (channels), enabling an analyst to "remove" one channel at a time, revealing what's left. You can literally "see" beneath the trees or below the ground, and that's quite a boost to archaeologists searching for the buried Holy Grail or the lost sixth ridge.[67]

When Paulette, the department secretary, buzzed that there was a guy named Tom calling from NASA in Bay St. Louis, I nearly spilled my coffee. Tom was a pioneer in the archaeological use of TMS/TIMS technology and had recognized the "invisible" Puebloan roads of Chaco Canyon. He had recently joined NASA, and here he was, on the phone with Earth—shaking news. "We just flew a mission over the Poverty Point site and wondered if you'd be willing to come over and take look at some of our new imagery. Like to get you to tell us what you see."

"Yeah, be happy to," I said, trying to act calm. "I've got classes tomorrow, but how about the day after? Tell me how to get there?"

Thus began our several-year-long collaboration. I examined the imagery at NASA and attended a workshop he hosted on TMS/TIMS archaeological application. Tom came to our digs at Poverty Point several times and lectured to our annual pilgrimages. It was during one of his visits to Poverty Point that we realized the potential of some of the data revealed by the spectacular colorized imagery.

Tom had given me a set of polaroid prints of several TIMS images, and after overcoming their mesmerizing artistic allure and conducting a detailed comparison, I spotted "anomalies" on one of the images. They weren't visible on the other prints. I mixed the anomalous picture in with the other Polaroids and spread them all out on the counter in the old lab at Poverty Point.

Tom had lectured on the new technology at the dorm the night before and was cheery, despite having stayed up Johnny Carson–late with some of our own night owls. K.B.'s biscuits had revived him, along with his second cup of twice-dripped Community coffee. In addition, another distinguished visitor had just poked his head in the door—George was an archaeologist with the National Geographic Society and had dropped by en route back to

A thematic mapper simulator (TMS) image of Poverty Point from 1982. Onion rings are not shown on these data bands. *Polaroid photograph provided courtesy of Thomas Sever (NASA).*

Washington to see Poverty Point up close. I later found out he had another motive—someone had told him about the down-home country cooking at Buddy and Peggy's little café in Epps, and he was anxious to try it.

Following handshakes, pleasantries and the sparkle of pocket camera flashes coming from the surge of students pushing into the lab, we managed to make our way to the counter with the images. Funny—everybody wanted to work in the lab that day, whereas most days, finding lab staffers was like searching for a sugar cube on Destin's white sand beaches.

"Hey, Tom, why don't you and George check out these pictures and see if you see anything unusual." Their inspection lasted all of fifteen seconds.

"Are you talking about this row of circles?" Tom asked.

"Yep."

"Can we go look at them on the ground?"

"Let me grab the soil probe out of the truck, and we'll walk up there. It's not far. The spot's already been flagged."

The lab emptied, and everybody moved along the narrow tram road, toward the flagged location in the plaza, just inside the innermost ring in the northern part of the enclosure.

"So much for the flags," I said, watching the bushhog turn around along the flank of the innermost ring where the flags used to be. "I forgot today was mowing day. Oh well, doesn't matter, I remember where I set 'em."

"Y'all might better wait here on the tram road 'til Blondel gets through mowing," Dennis grinned. "She takes no prisoners."

For years, Poverty Point's groundkeepers accentuated the concentric rings, which some tourists had trouble seeing from ground-level, by planting red clover on their crests. Even after the color faded, the clover, by then knee-high, continued to make the rings stand out, especially when park staff regularly kept the grass mowed in the bordering plaza and in the ditches between the rings. Today was grass-cutting day.

Blondel and Big Robert were the chief mowers, and it was Blondel's turn today. With blond hair flying, she sat proudly on the John Deere tractor, red paisley handkerchief pulled up over her nose and streaks of white sunscreen on her cheeks. She looked like a painted shield maiden headed into battle. Blondel and her mount only knew one speed, wide-open. Flying up and down her mowing lanes, trailing a cloud of dust and clippings, she barely braked on reaching the end of the mowing lanes along the inner ring at opposite ends of the enclosure. Instead, she wheeled the tractor in a tight turn, causing the bushhog to skip along the ground and fling the clippings accumulated on top in a sweeping circle.

After Blondel moved to the other side of the state highway, Dennis stood up and, making an exaggerated show of wiping his brow and sighing with feigned relief, said, "I think we're safe now. Bet you're glad you stayed on the tram trail."

"Smell that?" Thomas asked. "Didn't know there was a McDonald's around here."

"That's no McDonald's," disputed biology major Darrell. "It's wild onions."

Sure enough, when we walked out onto the freshly mowed plaza, we noticed the dark-green cuttings from aromatic wild onions. They were strewn everywhere across the entire northeastern section of the plaza, except along the turn row paralleling the base of the inner ring, where the flagging had been placed.

"Doc, you want us to get the soil probe and start taking cores?" asked James.

"Looks like that won't be necessary," I frowned, noticing that the dark green rings coincided with the turning circles of Blondel's bushhog. "There's nothing buried out here. Looks like we've been chasing after onion rings."

"Too bad, Tom, I thought we were really onto something, like buried house rings or old cane-grinding mills, something."

Tom thought for a minute, "Oh well, at least we know TMS can distinguish wild onions from red clover."

"Come on, you guys," said George. "We need to get to Buddy and Peggy's if you still want me to give a talk on our research at Dzibilchaltun this afternoon.[68] I've got to catch a plane at 6:00 p.m."

An afterthought: the infrared imagery had captured wild onions sprouting from cuttings spread in circles by the previous month's mowing. We just happened to be present on a day when Blondel was actually creating future onion rings. Had it been any other season, we would still be puzzling over these ephemeral features.

THREE AMIGOS AND A GHOST

After a hearty Betty and Gloria–cooked supper, three friends decided to hike to the Great Mound just as the sun was setting. Becky, Mary and Kathleen walked vigorously around the park road on the lookout for foxes, kites, cicadas and any of the totem animals of Poverty Point. As they neared the Great Mound, the girls stopped to take a photograph. "Smile, you hussies," beamed Kathleen.

"Who's a hussy? You're the one that said that if you ever found a man that did feet as well as you can, you'd marry him," exclaimed Becky.

"Yeah, bet you got 'em all signed up for massage lessons," Mary chimed in.

With the picture taken and camera returned to backpack, the girls resumed their two mile-trek around the road. Tommy was waiting for them at the dorm.

"Where you amigos been?" he beamed. "Kathleen, will you rub my aching feet now?"

"No, Tommy, I will not do your feet. Why don't you go wash some PPOs or something?"

Some days later, the girls picked up the developed photographs at the Epps' drugstore. Rushing back to Poverty Point, they hurried to the picnic table, where several of us were contemplating the price of cotton.

"You gotta see this!"

The photograph clearly showed three people: Becky, Mary and a third indistinct figure standing behind them. Kathleen had taken the picture. The figure was faint but seemed to be that of a man.

"Got to be light coming through the lens."

"Could be an emulsion problem or maybe a reflection of some kind."

"What y'all talking about?" Art grumbled. "It's a ghost. This is Poverty Point."

This was no *shilombish*, but then, maybe this ghost was not that of a Native.

No Photos Allowed, Part 1

For a long time, there have been rumors about strange outcomes involving picture taking at Poverty Point. The story of the three amigos is but one. All the incidents recalled here involved experienced photographers and old-fashioned film cameras. At the time the photographs were taken, the weather and lighting conditions were perfect, and the photographers were in good health, of sound mind and completely sober.

On occasion, it seems that Poverty Point simply does not want its picture taken. One memorable incident took place during the 1988 field school. A photographer from the *New York Times* who was visiting the excavation decided to take some pictures from Sarah's Mount located on the first ring in the southeastern corner of the ringed enclosure. He shot two rolls of film with two different cameras, and both rolls turned out blank. His ensuing letter expressed dismay and amazement, especially since both cameras worked perfectly fine away from Poverty Point. As if to make the curious event more curious, the roll of film I took of the photographer taking pictures also turned out blank. Afterward, my old

Minolta functioned flawlessly, and the Kodak Gold 200 film produced high-quality prints.

Sometimes, Poverty Point offers no simple explanation.

NO PHOTOS ALLOWED, PART 2

Ten years after the incident with the *New York Times* photographer, there was another glitch with a would-be photographer. This incident involved John Turner, an editor of the *West Carroll Gazette*. Turner was seeking an item for the newspaper on the ongoing excavations being conducted by a combined team of students from the University of Southwestern Louisiana and Northeast Louisiana University. Turner was also to discuss some of the finds with Bob, the state regional archaeologist stationed at Poverty Point and the expedition coleader. He was particularly intrigued by two items that had been found:

> *The clay figurine, which appears to be an owl* [sic] *and the steatite pendant are what proved interesting at the end of my visit.*
>
> *Efforts to photograph these objects were fruitless.*
>
> *The staff removed the glass case from the display so I could get a picture. The camera would not snap.*
>
> *Dr. Connolly held one of objects up in his hand so the camera would be level. It would not snap. He held it in other positions. The camera would not snap.*

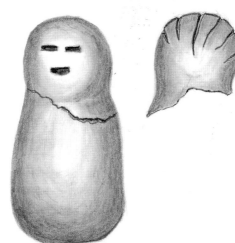

A photograph stopper, a reproduction of small earthenware human figurine recovered from Poverty Point's upper west sector. Note the hairdo. *Drawn by Jon Gibson.*

I pointed the camera away from the object. It snapped. I aimed it back at the artifact. It would not snap. Pointed away, it snapped—again. We tried with no success, until he held one of them up, and I shot from the hip, more or less, guessing at the aim—it snapped.

But before we get something started, let me point out that one of the staff members said she had no trouble with her camera.

Maybe the owl and the pendant just didn't want their picture in the paper.[69]

A drawing of the figurine appears on page 97. I had no trouble taking a picture of the figurine, but I must admit, the picture was of a molded reproduction and not the real thing.

UFOLOGIST AND THE POVERTY POINT OBJECT

John Calhoun recalls an incident involving Mitchell and a noted ufologist.

Erich von Daniken, author of the much-publicized Chariots of the Gods had visited Poverty Point doing research for an article for National Enquirer or some other such tabloid. Apparently, he was going to make Poverty Point an ancient space port. Von Daniken's theories have been widely embraced by the yellow press and starry-eyed people who have talked with aliens, visited Atlantis and lived past lives.

Mitchell, never one to miss a golden opportunity, led von Daniken into the lab and showed him a conical cooking object with cane impressions.... It took very little imagination to equate the shape of the object to an Apollo space capsule and interpret the circular cane impressions as port holes. Mitchell chuckled and told me that von Daniken ran out of the lab… convinced that he had conclusive proof that Poverty Point was a three-thousand-year-old interstellar landing site.[70]

A few other details about von Daniken's theory come to mind. Mitchell told me that von Daniken locked onto the landing site idea the instant he saw the ephemeral, water-filled depression behind the Great Mound. Von Daniken was convinced it had been gouged out by thrusters of a giant starship. However, other explanations for the depression suppose a mundane origin. One suggests that it was a Native borrow pit, another, a partially filled-in Pleistocene stream channel. And these accounts may not

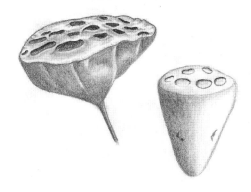

An American lotus seed pod (*left*) and "space capsule" PPO (*right*). Rhizomes were a food staple for Poverty Point people and grow in shallow, still-water bayous, sloughs and lake margins. The presumed "space capsule" PPO fuels ufologist's theory that Poverty Point was a spaceship's landing site. A cone-shaped earthenware object with bamboo cane impressions on a flat face. *Drawn by Jon Gibson.*

be mutually exclusive. Pollen and soil studies confirm it has been a slough for a long time—at least as long as abutting landforms. Yet, they are silent about its origin.

Then there is the matter of von Daniken's supposed "space capsule." It is not one of the typical earth-bound Poverty Point objects, but it is obviously an effigy of an American lotus seed pod.[71] The lotus is an aquatic plant with woody cone-shaped seed pods. Pods are about as big as a fist, and each holds a score or more hard-shelled seeds in individual cup-like receptacles.

Both seeds and rhizomes are edible, and based on slim evidence, lotus rhizomes seem to have been an important, maybe even primary, food source at Poverty Point. Such a bold declaration is based on seven PPOs— that's right, a grand total of seven out of multiple millions, a percentage so miniscule that five zeros lie to the right of the decimal before a significant number appears. It's a small sample, but it is compelling; that's the key, like the omnipresence of iridium in the KPg boundary or nanodiamonds in the Younger Dryas black mats.

Paleobotanist Linda Cummings analyzed the microscopic residue on thirteen indiscriminately grabbed PPOs and found lotus starch on seven of them.[72] Now, it's true, we don't know how representative these seven are of Poverty Point's overall economy at any given moment in its long history, but it's hard not to imagine that if lotus starch showed up on more than half of any old double-handful of PPOs, lotus must have been a common food, if not a staple.

RECLUSE ROULETTE

You would have thought the long line of slow-moving cars leaving the parking lot was going to a funeral. It was not. It was bound for Lafayette, the university home of most of the students who had just wrapped up field school at Poverty Point.

A handful of us sat on the picnic table in front of the dorm, waving and trying to suppress the melancholy that was already beginning to settle into the void left by their departure. Fogie, 'Houn, Lisa, Greg, Fred, Karon, Kathy, Erin and Yvonne stayed behind. On Monday, we would start another dig at the Francis Thompson Site on Bayou Macon, some fifteen miles south of Poverty Point. The official purpose of our dig was to determine its eligibility for the National Register of Historic Places, but our private research interests focused on figuring out how it fit within the greater Poverty Point scheme of things, archaeologically, socially and historically.[73] Plus, we had loose ends to tie up at Poverty Point before we could put the field school to rest.

Aside from the noisy owls, the nighttime quiet came early. Muted voices replaced the usual banter in the commons area of the dorm, and it wasn't long before Fogie had resorted to playing solitaire. Before retiring, I stepped outside into the inky black that enveloped the world beyond the glow from the windows. Standing at the edge of the light, I heard the scurrying of tiny feet and the fluttering of winged "nit-nats" roused from their nocturnal roosts. Something large moved through the dogwood thicket, paused and then splashed across Harlin Bayou before leaving earshot. A cacophony of owl sounds—hoots, shrieks, barks, whistles and growls—animated the living night. Every owl in the parish seemed to have descended on Poverty Point. Was it *opa* or *shilombish* or both? There was no way to tell from the racket, but one thing was certain: the owl sounds were old, primitive and soulful.

First light found Fogie filling his coffee thermos, just as 'Houn—who always slept in his pickup—poked his head in the door and announced, "Trucks are packed, we're ready."

"What took y'all so long?" asked Yvonne. "We were just about to knock on the door. Doc, I'll bring my Trooper. It's got a winch in case you stick that citified Chevy. Lisa 's got the sandwiches, and Greg's got the cooler."

Mr. Ernest was waiting at the barbed-wire gate into the Thompson property. His four-by-four mud-caked Ford pickup stood tall atop narrow twenty-inch mud grips, a perfect answer for the just-dewatered quarter-mile-long run to the archaeological site. Mr. Ernest was the farm manager for the

Thompson properties. Since boyhood, he had negotiated these reclaimed swamplands by foot, tractor, truck, boat and sidestroke.

The team piled into the bed of his pickup for the ride in. The equipment rode in the other two trucks. If his pickup managed to reach the "island," the others would follow his track. With everyone hanging on like riders on a Tilt-A-Whirl, Mr. Ernest eased forward, and soon, all four wheels were slinging mud and water. Through the spray, we heard cheering and saw his truck mount the steep incline of the "island" where we were bound. They had made it with only a little mud in their eyes and pounding pulses to show for the exhilarating experience.[74]

Encouraged by the newly initiated cheerleaders, the Trooper and the Chevy four-by-four followed suit. On attaining the height, we climbed down from the trucks and scrutinized our surroundings. The "island" was, indeed, just that, a section of the Macon Ridge that had been cut off by an ancient course of the Arkansas River after the last ice age. The Macon Ridge was, itself, the remnant of an even older ice-age landform that been cut off from North Louisiana's uplands by still-older ice melt waters of a then-combined Arkansas/Ouachita River.

The view was memorable:

> The island made an impressive sight, standing bold and denuded above the watery quagmire, semi-land, which, at other times of the year, was miraculously transformed into bean fields....It was large, covering about 17 acres....The top was flat and stood about four meters higher than the surrounding ground.
>
> I could sense why the Indians liked the place. Even surrounded by primeval forests, as it would have been before the White Man, visibility would have been good. A gentle southerly breeze stirred the humid air, unlike the unmoving layer which hung heavy over the swamp we had just crossed. Thinking of that led me to appreciate the solid ground now underfoot. Up here, the loess soil drained quickly; even wet, the dirt was not sticky. Sharkey clay is not like that.[75]

The next couple of days were spent laying off a grid for our excavation and controlled surface collecting. We experienced nothing out of the ordinary, unless you consider a mother coyote moving her pups farther out into the swamp as being extraordinary. After our daily work at the Francis Thompson Site, the team returned to Poverty Point and finished digging the Robert Parrish Test Pit, which had not been completed when field school ended.

Named after an early Depression-era farmer, the pit was placed on the high point of one of the rings where his house had stood.[76] There was nothing out of the ordinary there either, unless you consider finding proof that the elevation was architecturally part of the ancient ring rather than a separately added mound to be extraordinary. So far, everything was going smoothly.

So, it came to pass that our gang happily accepted Francis's invitation to a fish fry at his camp on Joe's Bayou. Aside from the good food and good company, it was nice to have the youngsters' hard work appreciated. That's when I felt the pain in my foot, and by the time I saw the doctor in Delhi next morning, my foot was swollen so badly my toes were barely visible. The initial diagnosis was a brown recluse bite. The Delhi clinic made arrangements for treatment at a Monroe hospital. My daughter Erin took the I-20/U.S. 165 flight path to the hospital, where I was apprehended by a squad of staffers in blue scrubs armed with large needles, plastic garrotes and a wheelchair with arm restraints. As it turned out, the real culprit was not a spider but blood poisoning. Three days later, my wife, Mary Beth, and Erin chauffeured me back to the Poverty Point dorm, where we were greeted by a banner on the front door that read, "Sanitized for your Safety, Thank You, The Management."[77]

The brown recluse scare precipitated an intensive spider hunt and led to the creation of one of the most notable gaming platforms in the history of Poverty Point's trivial pursuits. Fearing the dorm was a recluse sanctuary, Dennis and gang began prepping it for fumigation. The idea of Recluse Roulette was born in the passion of that day. The rules were simple: (a) douse spider with insecticide; (b) place bets on whether or not movement ceases within a ten-second span; (c) pot goes to winner who picks correct outcome; (d) if there is no winner, the pot carries forward until next round, and next, et cetera, or until a single wagerer picks the correct outcome.[78]

Scores of spiders, including venomous brown recluses, were exterminated in those fateful hours, and scores of quarters wound up in the pocket of master gamer Fogie. In a later interview, winner Fogie admitted, "I've always been lucky. I think it comes from having grown up in a parish named after a saint."

The Raffman Affair

One off-day during the 1983 field season, I was busy with a pile of paperwork when Mitchell poked his head in the lab door. "Come on," he mumbled, "let's go." I could tell by the gleam in his eyes that he had something special in mind, but I didn't ask him where we were going. I knew he wanted me to figure that out myself.

We piled in his old '71 Chevy pickup and slow-poked our way south, toward Christine's little store, where we stopped to pick up Nehi oranges and peanut butter crackers. We crossed over the iron bridge across Bayou Macon and headed south toward Monticello. When Mitchell turned off the highway and onto the Panther Lake gravel, I knew where we were headed—Raffman.

Mysterious Raffman was a lost mound site hiding in the hardwood "jungles" of the Tensas swamp, a dozen or so miles from Poverty Point. Legendary archaeologists Stu and Phil had chased down the overgrown site several years before, and Stu described it thusly: "Had a whopping big flat-top [mound] surrounded by five other pretty good-sized mounds, and possibly a fortification."[79]

For years, Mitchell and I talked about visiting Raffman but were never able to work out the logistics. Now, here we were, parked along the narrow shoulder of the road fronting the huge tract of old-growth forest where the mounds lay hidden—literally.

A bird's-eye view of Raffman during its heyday. *Drawn by Jon Gibson.*

We would have to walk the rest of the way. A huge mudhole blocked the turn-in to the dim trail leading to the site. Besides, the truck tires were slick, and we had no "come-along." After dousing ourselves with Off, we plunged into thick dark woods.

The sensory transformation was immediate, just like someone had just turned off the light. As our eyes adjusted to the darkness, we began to appreciate the primordial majesty of the old-growth forest—giant trees towering 120 feet overhead, bracket fungus growing thickly on fallen giants and decaying limbs and the blanket of ferns hiding the ground and its army of reptiles—well, not all remained hidden. We carefully made our way around a canebrake rattler that had found a small sunlit spot on the trail and refused to budge, its whirring tail warning us where not to step. Thick-bodied, musty-smelling cottonmouths did yield, but we knew they didn't slither very far away. A bullfrog croaked from a hidden slough to the right, and a hyla chorus came out of the buttonbushes that lined its banks. And the smells—the damp rotting wood, the sweet buttonbush flowers and the septic mud puddles—invaded the consciousness and completed the sensory transformation set in motion by the perpetual dusk in the forest.

The mood-altering effect of the dank woods became more profound as we moved deeper into them. After leaving the croaking frogs behind, the silence grew heavier. We both sensed the change and stopped talking. We felt like we had left civilization behind and were traveling down a trail that led back in time. I don't think either of us would have been surprised to see a *nalusa falaya* step out from behind the huge oak tree, which loomed on the incline immediately ahead.

As we stepped onto the incline, we realized it was the steep slope of a towering mound. "This thing's humongous. Bet it's bigger than the high school gym, and look, there's another one over yonder. Stu said there were five mounds, but I can see six or seven from here," I observed, peering through the thick cane. "Man, we should'a brought the big tape."

"Humh, should'a brought machetes and swing blades," Mitchell grunted. "Couldn't'a pulled a tape more'n three feet in any direction without clearing lines."

A horned owl hooted nearby, sending chills up our damp jeans' legs, but when her mate quickly answered from a neighboring tree, we breathed a collective sigh of relief. Thank goodness, these were real owls and not malicious *shilombish* warning of a pending death. We paused for a breather and swallowed our peanut butter crackers.

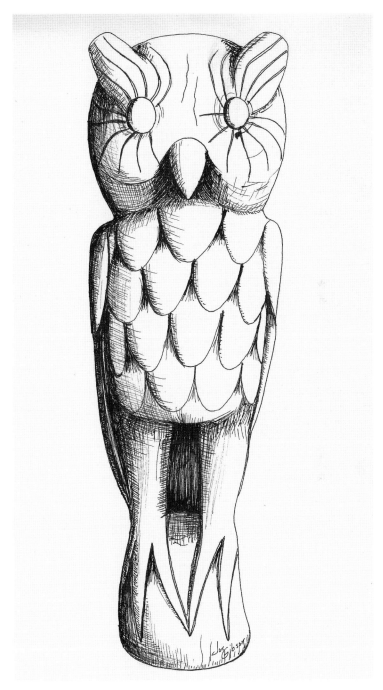

A great horned owl totem. Anonymous carver, donated by Leslie Delaney. *Drawn by Jon Gibson.*

"You know," said Mitchell, "old-timers tell me this is where Teddy Roosevelt camped when he came to Louisiana to hunt bears. S'posed to be an old dilapidated cabin somewhere 'round here where he stayed. Said he came here to meet up with a fella name of Ben Lilly, an old bear hunter who lived in these parts. Lilly was his guide 'cause, let me tell you, this was wild-ass country back then. It was all virgin woods everywhere, wasn't no paved highways or wet-weather roads. Everything was underwater half the year, 'cept for old Indian trails up on the highest levees. Folks mainly traveled on the rivers. Rumor has it that Roosevelt killed so many bears that his people had to clear a whole acre of trees just to build skinning racks. Now, I don't know about that, but they tell me Lilly left Louisiana right after the Roosevelt hunt and went out west somewhere, became a modern-day mountain man."

That's when we spotted the movement high up in the big tree and heard the bark fall.

"What's that?" I whispered. My mood had definitely been altered, but I fervently hoped reality hadn't—the image of a *nalysa falaya* behind the tree was still very vivid. Through an opening in the dense foliage, we saw the bear cub slide down the tree trunk, followed quickly by her sibling. Mitchell and I looked at each other, struck by the same ominous question: "Where's mama bear?" No gun, not even a pocketknife, and both of us sadly out of shape if it came down to a foot race. We didn't have to wait long for our answer to scramble down the tree, pause at the opening long enough to leer at us with her beady black eyes and then shinny down the last forty feet of tree so fast you'd thought she was in free fall.

She hit the ground running, and hearing her crashing through the canebrake brought out another primitive instinct in Mitchell and me—fear, sheer, unadulterated, unconstrained fear.

"Run!" The alarm was shouted by every fiber of our beings except for our vocal cords, which weren't working properly. And run we did, back along the dim trail, hurdling limbs and bushes and snakes and mud puddles until we sprawled headlong into a tangled fern glen. Out of breath and exhausted, we hid behind an old brick pile to see if we could hear her coming and prepare ourselves in case we had to make a last stand.

"She's still chasing us," I thought. My ears were pounding loudly, like heavy footfalls close by—too close. I considered lying on my stomach, which was what I'd always heard you were supposed to do in a bear attack, but then I didn't want her chewing on my behind either. Slowly, the heavy pounding began to abate, and I realized I had been hearing my heart beating heavily in my ears. The woods fell eerily silent. We couldn't hear the bear. She must be nearby, we thought, stalking us, readying her attack. Steeling myself, I rose, picked up a limb, broke it into club length and resigned myself to meet fate head-on. I intended to go out fighting. Mitchell, armed with his own stout shillelagh, turned to face the trail. "Come on, bear, get a taste of some hickory."

After a few more anxious moments, Mitchell whispered, "I can't hear her anymore, reckon she's gone?" Near-calm replaced fright, and when we had time to think rationally about our booger-bear, we realized she was a black bear and was probably as frightened by us as we were by her. Even with two cubs to protect, she was unlikely, we rationalized, to attack two full-grown men (later research showed that might not have been a safe assumption).

We retraced the path of our flight back toward the mounds, somewhat relieved but fully alert. We found the big tree, saw the claw marks in the bark and noticed the half-eaten muscadines around the exposed roots. And we found her trail through the trampled cane. It headed straight toward the river, opposite the direction we had fled in. She had never chased us; the pounding pursuer was our own fright.

We spent the rest of the day climbing each mound, pacing off and recording dimensions and tracing out what seemed to be an embankment encircling the plaza on the side away from the river. We even found a few pieces of pottery in a deer scrape. "Looks like Tchefuncte stuff to me," I opined, "Hum, that's odd. We don't think Tchefuncte people built big mounds around a plaza like this, but who knows for sure. You know, there are some pretty good Tchefuncte mound groups down around Lafayette on the Vermilion River. Now, they don't have great big mounds like these, or plazas, but then, their successors didn't either. We got Poverty Point over yonder, so they've got a pretty impressive precedent going for them up here."

Bear signs were everywhere, but no worry, our bravery and wood senses were restored, and our egos were largely patched up, although they remained somewhat fragile. The majesty of Raffman was the perfect sedative.

"Reckon we oughta be headin' out?" Mitchell asked as a red beam of light from the sinking sun illuminated the big mound where we were standing. I was caught between worlds—past and present—imagining the ancient rites that had been performed on this very same mound summit. The sentiment was powerful; I barely heard what he was saying.

"You know, 'em old hunters over at the cotton gin tell me their hounds have run deer in these woods and never come out again. Claim panthers got 'em." After the bear scare, mention of panthers got my full attention. I spoke then—rather too quickly, I suspect.

"Yep, reckon it's time to be getting back, getting late, sun's almost down."

Raffman's magic was quickly fading into ominous darkness. We headed back down the dim trail toward the truck, using Mitchell's Zippo the last quarter mile to light the way. If Mitchell noticed any quickening in my step on the way back, he didn't say anything, but he stayed right by my side the whole way.

It was dark-thirty when we got back to Poverty Point. I grabbed my backpack, slid out and slammed the truck door. The worn-out latch caught this time. Mitchell wheeled the truck around and drove out of the parking lot.

"Yep," he called out, nodding as he passed by.

"Yep," I returned the gesture.

Long after my head hit the pillow, I lay awake, not worried about snakes or booger-bears, but wondering about whether Poverty Point or Raffman had the blackest nights.

(As an aside, the Raffman works were not Tchefuncte constructions. Instead, they were built by local Coles Creek folk one thousand years later.)[80]

6

STORIES FROM VISIONARIES AND BIOLOCATORS

Some stories about Poverty Point do not spring from Native folklore or from archaeology teams caught up in Poverty Point's mysteries. Modern-day visionaries and visitors with special sensory receptivity also pick up on Poverty Point's extraordinary emanations. The following are some of their visions.

MOUND A AND THE OLD KINGDOM

Back in the 1970s, I was attending an antiquities commission meeting in Baton Rouge. The hot topic of the day had to do with the so-called Tunica Treasure, a collection of grave goods illegally excavated from an eighteenth-century Tunica Native cemetery near Marksville.[81] But it was an item of new business that awakened my slumber. I've forgotten all the details, but the gist of the announcement was: "During a séance held in Baton Rouge…a group of visionaries remotely sensed beneath the big mound [at Poverty Point] a burial chamber appointed with Egyptian hieroglyphs and Old Kingdom furniture."[82]

Few archaeologists have ever "seen" what lies at the base of the big mound, and those who have—Jim and Stu; Bill; and T.R. and Tony—have been afforded only the tiniest of glimpses, either by means of a two-inch-wide auger barrel full of dirt or via a skin-thin, shovel-shaved profile exposure.[83] Despite obvious sampling limitations, none of these investigators encountered signs of mummies or Egyptian cartouches.

ANGELS AND DEMONS

On September 18, 1997, the *Banner-Democrat* newspaper of Lake Providence, Louisiana, reported that the Yap family, Pentecostal missionaries from Malaysia, were passing by Poverty Point in route to a revival in nearby Lake Providence when Mrs. Yap began to feel a darkness and hear wailing and moaning.[84] Mrs. Yap "knew" these emanations were due to Poverty Point having been a place of human sacrifice and great suffering. Her husband vouched for his wife's ability to "look into the spiritual realm and see angels and demons."

Evil emanations were not confined to Poverty Point, but they extended, though less powerfully, into the surrounding region, which was, according to Mrs. Yap, "a stronghold of satanic worship, witchcraft and black magic…so dense you can feel it." This revelation had come to her through divine inspiration.

The evil does not stop here either, she continued, but "is manifest throughout the nation of America."

"We must pray for America," she said.

And let's not forget Poverty Point. It is also included in consciousness studies expert and neo-alchemist Dennis Hauck's *The National Directory of Haunted Places.*[85]

LANDMARK TREE AND TOOTHPICKS

Before World War II, rural North Louisiana was Baptist country with a sprinkling of Methodists, Pentecostals and Presbyterians here and there. Roads converged on churches, and church families formed the heart of self-supporting communities. Churches were not merely places of worship, but venues for socializing and news sharing. I doubt if there's an elderly Native anywhere who didn't have at least one set of grandparents or great-grandparents who met, sparked and married at church. News flashes, such as old man Pickering's stolen hog or sister Grace Elaine's Dominicker hen laying double-yolk eggs, spread like a wildfire through dry weeds at Sunday services.

The Yaps' ominous message of debauchery and Satan worship reverberated through the church community. So, it came to pass that the Lake Providence preacher decided to go to Poverty Point to pray. Just as Moses ascended Mount Sinai, he climbed the Great Mound and knelt at the foot of the old oak tree on its summit.

The old tree was a landmark. It had weathered countless storms, a remarkable feat considering it was the highest point for miles around, a veritable lightning rod that challenged mighty *Mela'tha* over the years and won. It was revered by psychics, and its exposed roots offered seating for many a breathless mound climber. Its hidden cavities presented "double-dog-dare-you" challenges to local children who poked their hands into their dark recesses inhabited by all manner of unseen creepy-crawlies and unnatural things. One of its overhanging limbs anchored the winch used by archaeologists Jim and Stu to lower and extract the soil auger from the sixty-foot-deep borehole that first confirmed the mound was constructed rather than natural.[86] It hosted innumerable summit meetings and nighttime gatherings, and it shaded the lofty viewing stage where goings-on below could be best observed.

The devout preacher prayed that good would overcome evil and that salvation would come to his congregation and their brothers and sisters. His piety bode well for repentance and healing.

A few days later, a line of angry thunderstorms marched across the land from the northwest. *Mela'tha* hurled his mighty lightning spear like he had thousands of times before, but this time, it struck the landmark tree, traversed its furrowed trunk and dug into the ground. There, it exploded with a blinding flash and blast that was seen and heard only by the mound's denizens.

Even Dennis, who lived nearby, was unaware of the incident until he saw white smoke arising from the crater the next morning. Dennis said the explosion was so powerful that it obliterated the whole tree. "I never saw anything like it in my life," he said, the astonishment still evident in his voice after three decades. "Wadden' nothing left but toothpicks—nothing for the ground crew to pick up. We built a small observation deck over the crater."

Dennis thought for a moment. "I'll tell you, I'm not going to try to second-guess why the tree was struck or why it blew up so completely, but it does make you wonder why it happened only days after the good preacher's prayer when it had stood unscathed for all these years." No kidding.

Poverty Point and the New Atlantis, Part 1

In a fanciful depiction of Poverty Point, Frank Joseph draws attention to its "remarkable" resemblance to Plato's description of the capital of the sunken continent of Atlantis.[87] Namely, both places had concentric rings of alternating land and water connected by canals; Atlantis had Mount Atlas, a volcano, and Poverty Point had Mound B, a "symbolic volcano." Both places recurrently used the numbers five and six, sacred numbers representing male and female energies, and both places were "hubs of trading empires joined by water routes."[88] Joseph avers that Poverty Point was founded by reincarnated Atlanteans or refugees who rebuilt their new city "in the image of their drowned capitol." He finds compelling "proof" of Atlantean origin in the readings of Edgar Cayce, a renowned psychic.

Joseph envisions Poverty Point as a sacred power center that ignites "past-life regressions for persons of all backgrounds—but especially for reincarnated Atlanteans."[89] He provides easy-to-follow instructions for a successful vision quest: (a) absorb land and water energies by walking across the concentric rings; (b) be particularly attuned to receiving flashbacks of past lives while crossing the fifth and sixth rings, where gender energies are released; (c) ascend the Great Mound and perform a water ritual at the base of the magnificent oak tree on the mound's summit; (d) proceed northward, toward the Mound B power point, where another water ritual may help invoke a vision; and (e) return to museum across the rings and plaza, the city's hub where sun movements were once charted.[90]

Joseph elaborates on the important parts of the water ritual. First, the visionary should face east, pour out a swig of purified water and thank the *genius loci* for permitting the visit. He should then face south and repeat the gesture and continue clockwise until all four directions have been wetted and thanked.

He identifies the Great Mound as the "chief spiritual focal point" of new Atlantis and the oak tree on top as the "lightning rod" for all the city's energies.[91]

> [T]*he oak was a manifestation of Atlas, whose arms upheld the sphere of the heavens. It is the Tree of Life at the Atlantean sacred center of the world, the living axis mundi, replanted by the gods at its most perfect spot. Powerful meditation and/or past life regression are wonderfully facilitated beneath its numinous branches.*[92]

Unfortunately, the ritual can no longer be performed as instructed. The ancient oak tree, which, according to Joseph, had been "replanted by the gods" from the acorns of its submerged counterpart, was blown apart in a thunderstorm.

Was Zeus unhappy with Atlas, or was *Mela'tha* merely flapping his wings?

We lack firsthand access to clairvoyant insight on Atlantean resettlement, but there may be a link between Poverty Point and Santorini. Some theories point to Plato's Atlantis being the ancient Minoan capital on the island of Thera (Santorini), which sunk into the Mediterranean Sea during a cataclysmic volcanic eruption. Radiocarbon dates indicate the disaster occurred around 1600 cal. BCE, or maybe a few decades afterward. Poverty Point's first mound, Mound B, was constructed around 1628 cal. BCE.[93] A coincidence half a world away? It's unlikely. We expect that fallout from the Santorini eruption created a long-lasting worldwide winter, responsible for the pluvial conditions that existed when Poverty Point was founded.[94]

How the cold, rainy weather and megaflooding, which likely persisted for years or decades, contributed to Poverty Point's onset and subsequent expansion is unknown and may not be knowable, but this much has been learned: there was never some uniform, global cultural response to the cold and wet, but hunter-gatherers everywhere seem not to have been as economically stressed by raw weather conditions as farmers were.[95] There are indications that Poverty Point's economy and technology were finely geared to the wild foods of river swamps, possibly to the point of dependency on year-round fishing and aquatic root collecting. Still, the crux of the matter is not so much about a general economic shift as it is about those influential historical figures who led the way and resolved the social tensions that arose.

POVERTY POINT AND THE NEW ATLANTIS, PART 2

Lost continent proponent John Ward, in his 1984 book *Ancient Archives Among the Cornstalks: Twenty-Seven Century Old Documents on Stone Revealing a Commercial Enterprise of Mediterranean Colonists in the Wabash Valley of MidAmerica*, also maintains that Poverty Point was the New Atlantis, founded by Atlantean refugee-entrepreneurs seeking to mine valuable lead ore deposits in the Upper Mississippi Valley.[96]

It makes you wonder why traders didn't settle closer to the pit mines in the Upper Mississippi Valley. They could have saved time and energy, as lead ore (galena) circulated far and wide along the Mississippi River and its tributaries.[97] Here's another thought: there is a twelve-century hiatus between the first round of galena trade, which Ward attributes to the Atlanteans, and a second wave of galena trade that spanned much of the same network. Were these later galena peddlers blood descendants of the Atlanteans? If so, how did they manage to hold on to their distant grandfathers' legacies without leaving leaden traces all over the intervening centuries? Why would they have wanted to resurrect a long-dead livelihood anyway?

The answer? They were not, they could not and they did not.

EARTH SIGNS AND BIOLOCATION

In a paper presented to the Society for Scientific Exploration, Andrei Apostol (2002), a New York geophysicist, proposed an interesting theory dealing with the cooccurrence of North American effigy mounds and geophysical anomalies. He included Poverty Point in his baseline because, at the time, the Great Mound was presumed to be a bird effigy, the oldest representational mound in mainland North America.[98] The impetus for his investigation came from discoveries that showed some prominent Mesoamerican centers, such as Teotihuacan, Chichen Itza and La Venta, were associated with caves and/or subterranean oil pools and, additionally, that Mesoamerican Natives generally ritualized caves, hot springs and fumaroles.

The Monroe gas rock and the Bouguer positive gravity and magnetic anomaly, one of the largest in Louisiana, directly underlie Poverty Point's location.[99] They resulted from the extensive breakup of the overlying sedimentary cap rock and resulting interpenetration by Cretaceous igneous rock "in the form of stocks, pipes, pipes, sills, intraformational flows and pyroclastics."

Apostol's study confirms the sympatry between Poverty Point's location and the underground anomalies, but if the association is not purely accidental and if the anomalies were the factor in siting Poverty Point, then the looming question becomes how in the world did Poverty Point's founders detect these deeply buried anomalies?

His bold answer is biolocation, the psychic ability for a person to remotely detect something or somebody that exists in a place apart from that of the observer. In order to test his theory that Poverty Point's location was chosen by psychically endowed Native shamans, Apostal recruited a German psychic with biolocator talents to see if he could remotely sense Poverty Point's underground anomalies. The blindfolded psychic was driven slowly along a country road, which crossed the mapped Bouguer gravity anomaly, and his responses were observed. Apostal reports that the psychic's muscles involuntarily tensed when he was over the anomaly and relaxed when he was not and that the strength of tension perfectly matched the shape of the gravity contours—stronger where the gravity was centered and weaker toward the edges.

How muscle tension was measured is unknown. It sounds like the psychic simply told Apostol how his arms felt when he passed each mile marker along the route. But word-of-mouth evidence is not scientific proof, and since no effort was made to independently reproduce the psychic's responses—

such as comparing the sensations of multiple bilocators driven along the same route—Apostol's claim must remain just that, an unconfirmed claim. Besides, even if the modern bilocator had successfully detected the gravity spike, it would not prove, in and of itself, that Poverty Point's location had been chosen by his prehistoric counterpart. There is no imaginable physical reason why an underground gravity anomaly would have been deemed important in site selection—say, any more than flood sanctuaries, plentiful and sustainable food sources or desirable social logistics networking. Even if a gifted seer had interpreted the sensory irregularity as a commandment from the Great Spirit or an edict from the ancestors, proof of the matter will not be found in science but in the realm of spiritualism or magic.

Verifiable scientific proof notwithstanding, Poverty Point is a sensationally unusual place, and the substantial body of folklore centered there vouches for the large number of people who have experienced that ambiance.

ONCE UPON A TIME
ON THE GREAT MOUND

These stories were recorded over a two-decade period during the 1980s and 1990s. I was an eye-witness or front-row listener to many of the storied events, and as the body of lore grew and Poverty Point's reputation as a place of mystery and power widened, visiting psychics and paranormal investigators began to tell of their own experiences. Mitchell and Dennis kept me abreast of their sensational accounts.

I sometimes wonder what it was about those times that drove the narrative. If similar stories were being told before or after, I am unaware of them, and there have been some champion raconteurs who left their archaeological marks on Poverty Point—namely, Bill, Stu and George. Were strange affairs simply going unnoticed or being ignored in the early days of investigations or afterward? Were they being shunned for fear of contaminating scientific purity or compromising investigator reputation?

I am sure some readers will regard these incidents as having no more meaning than seeing a butterfly in the rose garden or a pigeon in city park, but I also believe these observers would be oblivious to a four-hundred-pound "hog man" staring them in the face.[100] But then I readily admit that the strange and unusual are in the eye of the beholder.

Seems to me that the 1980s and 1990s were made ripe for stories by the involved personalities, especially one who was to become legendary himself—Mitchell, the fox-man.[101] The multitude of receptive field school students were preadapted to Poverty Point's sentience by being familiar with Native oral literature. It was the right place at the right time with the right people, no doubt helped along by the antics of the magical totem animals of Poverty Point—the owl, locust, fox, snake, woodpecker, kite and rabbit. On the other hand, there is no denying that some events are just downright odd, regardless of the timing or the observers' cultural backgrounds.

These events are now part of Poverty Point's history. Their narration has become as integral to telling the story of Poverty Point as earthworks, artifacts and radiocarbon dates. They are the modern-day counterparts of traditional lore passed down by ancient grandfathers around winter campfires.

Poverty Point is one of the most unique archaeological sites in America, north of Mexico. It has been called a puzzle, an enigma, and a singularity.[102] It has both defied explanation and been erroneously explained in accordance with ever-changing paradigms. Explanations come and go. Others, I am sure, are in the works, and some have yet to arrive from the Oort cloud.

Until someone changes the blackness of the nights, calms the breezes atop the Great Mound and removes the totem animals from the enchanted woods, Poverty Point will continue to intrigue and inspire future generations of receptive archaeologists and visitors. Long live the fox and the fox-man.

WORDS FROM THE GREAT MOUND

The following is a list of technical terms and Choctaw words used in the preceding stories. Definitions pertain to Poverty Point contexts.

acephalous community. A tribe, or co-residing group, lacking inheritable, hierarchical social positions and passed-down leadership roles; Poverty Point differs from simple tribes in having compelling, theocratic and ritualized authority in the form of a generation-spanning priesthood.

alidade. Primitive optical surveying instrument used in making contour maps; incorporates a telescopic sighting barrel mounted on a graduated stand; used to measure distance and calculate elevations, which are then transferred directly onto an underlying hand-inscribed contour map affixed to a plane table.

atlatl. Javelin thrower, a wooden hand-held lever with a hook end used to hurl stone-pointed javelins farther and faster than by hand.

Atuklant Illi. Land of the second death in the Choctaw afterworld; similar to the Hell of Christianity, but it is earmarked for souls of murderers only.

bakbak. Choctaw name for red-headed woodpecker.

bannerstone. Bilaterally symmetrical polished stone object with two wings or ears projecting from a central perforated or solid tube.

basic architectural unit. A Native large standard measure equaling fifty-two arm spans or eighty-six and two-thirds meters in today's metrics

Blue Goose. A name for Wade's old blue Dodge pickup truck.

Bouguer positive gravity and magnetic anomaly. An area of elevated gravity and magnetic readings resulting from subterranean irregularities in the underlying Paleozoic crust relative to the overlying modern land surface.

Bourré. A popular South Louisiana card game in which winners are determined by capturing the most tricks out of five "hands;" *bourré* is called when a player fails to win a single trick and must "match the pot."

cane-grinding mill. A horse-drawn contraption consisting of a log boom with one end attached to a central grinding wheel and the other end to a horse or mule; the animal walks in a circle, thus turning the grinder and squeezing the juice from the sugar cane that is being hand fed onto the loader surface. The juice is then boiled until it thickens, is strained and, *voila*, delicious cane syrup.

chimera. A composite creature composed of parts of different animals or of animals and humans; engravings at Poverty Point are typically of a part-human-part-owl or part-human-part-fox and may represent spirit beings, such as *shilombish* or *nalusa falaya*.

chula. The Choctaw name for the fox (*Vulpes vulpes*).

cosmic cycles. Recurring celestial periods, such as phases of the moon, equinoxes, solstices, yearly solar extremes or eclipses; distances between Poverty Point's mounds and other buildings represent day counts of various cycles (as depicted by the number of arm spans or larger units, equivalent to fifty-two arm spans).

domestic economy. The common everyday provisioning of food and other resources.

Dominicker. A large chicken with thick, dark-gray-light-gray-barred plumage.

earth-oven. A deep cone-shaped cooking pit where wrapped (insulated) foods are baked in a covered bed of preheated, hand-molded earthen objects called Poverty Point objects.

egalitarian society. A close-knit social body in which every person enjoys equal rights but not necessarily equal social standing; status differentiation is based on individual merit; usually refers to a group lacking a permanent centralized source of authority.

Footprint of the Year. In Yucatec Maya cosmology, this refers to the distance traversed by the rising sun along the horizon in forty days.

fox-man. A chimera combining elements of a man and a fox; represented by engravings on gorgets and plummets.

gorget. A flat, oval- or bar-shaped object fashioned of hematite, slate or channel coal; thought to have been worn around the neck as a shield, ornament or amulet or strapped onto the forearm as an arm guard or decorative band.

gradiometer. A surveying instrument that measures the slope of the earth's gravitational, or magnetic, field.

Grass Water Drop. The glowing heart of the Choctaw will-o'-the-wisp, which causes people to lose their way when seen; a light seen in the woods or swamps lacking an identifiable source.

Grecian key glyph. An engraving found on soapstone bowl consisting of repeated rectangular meanders forming a complex continuous line pattern; a single-line labyrinth.

ground-penetrating radar. A noninvasive geophysical device for imaging the subsurface using radar pulses; useful for detecting buried architectural features and artifacts.

Hashok Okwa Hui'ga. The Choctaw name for will-o'-the-wisp.

hog man. The vernacular name for the bigfoot creature reputed to live in the Corney Bayou bottoms of Claiborne Parish (Harris, 1,3); claimed to be eight-feet-tall, covered with long hair and feeds on feral hogs and wild game, which it kills and skins with long crooked teeth and claw-like fingernails.

Hula Popper. A topwater fishing lure designed to mimic a hopping frog when retrieved with a jerking motion.

hyla. Tree frogs.

iconography. Sacred images or symbols engraved on various stone objects or as small carved or hand-molded three-dimensional fired earthen figurines.

iridium. A platinum metal usually associated with meteoric impacts.

kashehotapala. The Choctaw name of a supernatural being, which is part-human and part-deer and revels in scaring hunters in the woods and in keeping children awake at night.

KPg boundary. A narrow stratigraphic layer separating the Cretaceous and Paleogene geological epochs, presumably created by an iridium-rich asteroid impact on the Yucatec Coast, which is believed to have caused the extinction of most life on Earth, including the dinosaurs.

Land of Ghosts. The Choctaw afterworld where souls of the dead who managed to find and cross the slippery entrance log and enter a happy, blissful existence; analogous to Christianity's Heaven.

ley line (way line). A straight alignment connecting two or more mounds or other important buildings, sometimes but not always corresponds to astronomical sightlines; Poverty Point's principal ley line, or prime meridian, is believed to represent a direct spiritual conduit between the ancestors and Poverty Point residents.

logistical exploitation (or logistical mobility). Economic strategy for providing food and other domestic resources by moving them to consumers rather than having consumers move to resources.

long-tail. A rare figure engraved on plummets, possibly represents an opossum (*Didelphis virginia*), an odd, dog-like marsupial animal with a hairless prehensile tail.

lotus. A flowering aquatic plant (*Nelumbo lytea*) with edible seeds and rhizomes; grows in still-water bayous, shallow lakes and flooded swampland around Poverty Point; important, possibly year-round, staple food for Poverty Point people.

lunar maximum. Refers to the most extreme northern and southern points tracked by the full moon as it progresses along the horizon during the year.

Marshalltown. The brand name for a popular pointing trowel used in hand-digging archaeological deposits.

mela'tha. The Choctaw word for lightning, envisioned as a giant male spirit bird that has the power to fell trees.

merged eternity glyph. An engraved cypher formed by two overlapping, figure-eight (identical to our mathematical eternity symbols) glyphs; comprises a single, continuous-line labyrinth.

midden. A soil layer organically enriched by discarded human garbage, or colloquially, any accumulation of trash.

moon. To the Natchez and other tribes, a moon represents the length of time between new moons; the Native solar year had thirteen "moons," twelve named lunar cycles and an unlucky five-day span.

Motley point. A javelin projectile point diagnostic of Poverty Point culture, featuring an elongated triangular body, barbed shoulders and stems with narrow necks and wide bases, usually chipped from imported gray Midwestern flint.

mudline. Weighted bottom strand of fishnet, or seine, designed to keep net unfurled while deployed in flowing water or while being dragged along a slough or lake bottom in a "roundup," an encirclement of netting around a fishing ground that is subsequently dragged ashore at a "haul bank," where ensnared fish are removed.

Muskhogean tribes. Several politically separate Southeastern Native groups who speak Muskogean languages; the Choctaw comprise one such group, and other Louisiana tribes, such as the Tunica, Natchez,

Chitimacha and Attakapa, spoke distantly related dialects, probably because they descended from a common ancestral mother tongue during the dim time.

nalusa falaya. The Choctaw name for long black being, a spirit being possibly represented by engravings on plummets and gorgets.

Nane' Chaha, Nanih Waiya. A sacred mound of the Choctaw Nation located in Winston County, Mississippi; considered the birthplace of the Choctaw people, their "Garden of Eden."

nanodiamonds. Diamonds less than a micrometer in diameter produced by a meteor impact or other high-energy explosion.

navels of the earth. Earthen mounds, viewed as symbols of human creation.

Northwestern. Northwestern State College, now Northwestern State University in Natchitoches, Louisiana.

old-growth forest. A virgin forest that has never been logged.

opa. The Choctaw name for the barred owl.

Opelousa catfish. A southern American vernacular name for the yellow, or flathead, catfish (*Pylodictis olivaris*); the best tasting of all catfish.

planing mill. The area of a sawmill where rough planks are passed through a wringer-like planer, which smooths and thins them to a uniform thickness; planing produces an incessant, high-pitched, ear-splitting scream, similar to that of a jet engine, only louder.

plummet. An oval- or teardrop-shaped net weight that usually has a grooved or perforated distal end made from heavy magnetite or hematite.

pneumatology. Broadly, the consideration of supernatural matters such as spirits, unseen powers, death and the afterworld.

political economy. Those aspects of making a living that involve interpersonal interaction or interaction with authority.

Poverty Point object (or PPO). A hand-shaped, fist-sized or slightly smaller earthenware object used to heat earth ovens; some oddly shaped or decorated objects may be representational or ideographic.

profile. The wall of an archaeological test pit or trench that has been cleaned and smoothed to reveal the stratigraphy and any subterranean human alterations.

radiocarbon date, calibrated. The estimated age of charcoal or other organic material in archaeological context determined by comparing the residual amount of radioactive carbon (^{14}C) with normal carbon (^{12}C); since ^{14}C begins to decay on cessation of respiration at a known half-life rate of 5,730 years, measuring the carbon ratio of a sample enables a conventional radiocarbon date to be calculated; conversion to "true" age, or calendar age, requires that the conventional date be calibrated by a scale that more closely represents independently recognized fluctuations in the atmospheric carbon reservoir.

rain cloud glyph. An engraving on a slate gorget that resembles a thunderstorm.

road of life. The allegorical journey of life, from birth to death, hypothetically represented by a convoluted single-path or single-line labyrinth.

sauce piquante. A wild game or seafood stew made with a spicy tomato-based roux.

shilombish. The Choctaw name for the Outside Shadow, one of a person's two souls, or ghost, which remains near its former home, scaring people and trying to make them leave; it assumes the form of the owl and the fox and can only be distinguished from them by not responding to the hooting or barking of their living counterparts.

shilup. The Choctaw name for the Inside Shadow, a person's second soul, which, on a person's death, immediately goes to the Land of Ghosts.

Shilip I Yokni. The Choctaw name for Land of Ghosts.

single-path labyrinth. A design etched on a soapstone vessel consisting of a convoluted path leading from a single starting point to a center; the path can be continuously followed without ever coming to a dead end or having to backtrack.

skate-key glyph. An engraving on plummets that resembles old-fashioned roller-skate keys continuously linked in a scroll encircling the body of a plummet.

Sonny's. A popular local honky-tonk.

standard unit of length (measure). A small Native uniform length used to plot distances between mounds and other buildings in Poverty Point and earlier cultures; equivalent to an arm span or approximately one and two-thirds meters in contemporary parlance.

stomp dance. A shuffle and foot-stamp dance carried out by Native costumed performers moving in a clockwise circle around an elevated square ground; the multiple earthen overlays comprising the early stages of the Plaza (Dunbar) Mound's platform resemble stomp dance grounds of historic Southeastern tribes, particularly the Creek.

Tchefuncte people. Prehistoric Natives of the Lower Mississippi Valley and adjacent coastline who lived during the early to late centuries of the first millennium before Christ; they were pragmatic fisher-shellfisher-hunter-gatherers who pioneered the use of low-fired pottery that often featured a suite of designs made by simple and drag-and-jab incising, rocker-stamping, fingernail impression-gouging and zoned punctuating.

Thematic Mapper Simulator, TMS. A satellite- or aircraft-borne optical system that maps the ground cover on the Earth's surface and enables human alterations to be "seen" from above.

Thermal Infared Multispectral Simulator, TIMS. A satellite- or aircraft-carried multispectral sensor that produces images of the Earth's surface in three visible light and four infrared spectra; electronically "deleting" one channel of spectral data or another enables the detection of previously "unseen" natural or cultural features on or beneath the earth's ground cover.

trace element analysis. Comparing concentrations (less than 1,000 ppm) of chemical elements found in rocks in order to determine if they came from the same outcrop or deposit; typically used by archaeologists to posit and characterize trade networks.

trail trade. Exchange carried out along overland trails rather than waterways; alternatively, since small portable zoomorphs are usually involved, this may track foot traffic between settlements.

tribalism. A strong sense of belonging to a kinship-based, decentralized society; Poverty Point society was likely tribal but incorporated a powerful theocratic lineage or lineages capable of temporarily acting as a centralized authority without having broad or long-lasting influence or enduring sanctioning powers.

woodhenge. At Poverty Point, a C-shaped enclosure (the open side corresponds to a steep bluff) of free-standing wooden posts and an outer-flanking ditch that was built before construction of the six concentric earthen rings; rings encircled the old dismantled wooden structure.

Younger Dryas black mats. Thin layers of black organic detritus that accumulated between 12,900 and 11,700 cal years ago as a result of returning cold climatic conditions due to global atmospheric fallout from a meteoric airburst or widespread burning from extensive volcanic eruptions.

zoomorphs. Carvings and engravings depicting animal forms, some realistic, such as fat-bellied owls and seashell pendants, and others are abstract, such as locust effigy beads and long-tail glyphs.

NOTES

Once Upon a Time

1. Gibson, "State Historic Site," 83–84.
2. Gibson, "Separating Sacred and Secular," 17–30.
3. Vaughn, "1988 Poverty Point," xx.
4. Doré, "Shaman's Crystal," xii.
5. Vaughan, "1988 Poverty Point," xx.
6. Gibson, "1993 Excavations"; Gibson, "1995 Excavations."
7. Calhoun, "Fox," 3–10; see "Vision of the Fox-Man" in this volume.

1. Poverty Point, An Archaeological Digest

8. Gibson, *Archaic Earthworks*, table 9.
9. Clark, "Surrounding the Sacred," 162–213; Gibson, *Archaic Earthworks*, 82–87; Patten, "Time and Distance."
10. *Missionary Herald*, 1828, 179–80, quoted in Swanton, *Source Material*, 196.
11. Paxton, *Cosmos*, 95–114.
12. Ford and Webb, "Poverty Point," 129; Willey and Phillips, *Method and Theory*, 156; Cummings, "Box 9.3.," 182–84; Jackson, "Adaptive Systems," 174–204; Shea, "Botanical Remains," 245–60; H. Ward, "Paleobotanical Record," 166–73.
13. Gibson, *Ancient Mounds*, 144–48.

14. Gibson, *Archaic Earthworks*, 174–75.
15. Clark, "Surrounding the Sacred," 162–213; Webb, "Culture," figures 27–29.
16. Gibson, *Ancient Mounds*, figures 9-2–9-3.
17. Gibson, "Separating Sacred and Secular," 26–30; Gibson, *Ancient Mounds*, 187–93.
18. Swanton, *Source Material*, 198.
19. Swanton, *Myths and Tales*, 21, 41, 199–200; Gill, *Religions*, 83–86.
20. Clark, "Surrounding the Sacred," 172–80; Patten, "Time and Distance."
21. Clark, "Surrounding the Sacred," 164.
22. Gibson, *Archaic Earthworks*, table 9.
23. Ibid., 175.

2. Stories Bearing Native Correspondence

24. Bushnell, *Choctaw*, 18.
25. Swanton, *Source Material*, 198.
26. Ibid., 199.
27. Bushnell, *Choctaw*, 18.
28. Swanton, *Source Material*, 199.
29. Bushnell, *Choctaw*, 33.
30. Moore, "Aboriginal Sites," 64; Ford and Webb, "Poverty Point," 18.
31. Gibson, "Earth Sitting," 226, figure 8.
32. Swanton, *Myths and Tales*, 42–52, 107–14, 159–62, 178, 203–11, 255–59.
33. Gibson, "1993 Excavations," ix–xi.
34. Swanton, *Indians*, 776.
35. Calhoun in Gibson, "1993 Excavations," xiv.
36. Pitchlynn in Swanton, *Source Material*, 218.
37. Gibson, "Sixth Ridge."
38. See "*Bakbak* and the Chosen Test Pit, Parts 1 and 2" in this volume.

3. Locust Stories

39. Webb, "Locust Beads," 105–14.
40. Brookes, "Cultural Complexity," 108–9; Connaway, "Keenan Bead Cache," 57–81; Crawford, "Effigy Beads."
41. Wright, "Choctaws," 182.

42. Hunter, "Cicada," 222.
43. Swanton, *Source Material*, 10–11.
44. Bushnell, "Myths," 527.
45. Swanton, *Social Organization*, 63–64.
46. Gibson, *Archaic Earthworks*, 33, figure 18.
47. Hunter, "Cicada," 219–26; Webb, "Locust Beads," 105–14; Bushnell, "Myths," 526–35.

4. Fox Stories

48. Campbell, "Afterworld," 146–54; Swanton, *Source Material*, 170–93.
49. Campbell, "Afterworld," 146–54; Wright, "Choctaws," 182.
50. Wright, "Choctaws," 182.
51. Ibid.
52. Gibson, "Sixth Ridge," v.
53. Webb, "Fox-Man," 6–7.
54. Calhoun, "Fox," 3–10; Gibson, "Mitchell Hillman," 253–67.
55. Calhoun, "Fox," 3–10.
56. Johnson, "Yazoo Basin," 59–64.
57. Vaughan, "1988 Poverty Point," xx.
58. Mueller, *Sampling*; Renfrew and Bahn, *Archaeology*, 75–76.
59. Calhoun, "Fox," 8–9.
60. Gibson, "Earth Sitting," 213.

5. Human Interest Stories

61. Cushman, *History*, 215.
62. Swanton, *Source Material*, 203, 205.
63. Ibid., 210.
64. Ford, "Additional Notes," 282–85.
65. Hargrave and Clay, "Interim Report"; Ellerbe and Greenlee, *Poverty Point*, 46–52.
66. Mayer, "Appendix D," 213, figure D3.
67. Gibson, "Sixth Ridge."
68. Stuart and Stuart, *Lost Kingdoms*.
69. Turner, "Strange Things."
70. Calhoun, "Fox," 8.

71. Ford and Webb, "Poverty Point," 39–44, figures 13–14.
72. Cummings, "Box 9.3.," 182–84.
73. Gibson, "Island in the Past," 5–11.
74. Calhoun in Gibson, "Island in the Past," iv–v.
75. Gibson, "Island in the Past," 3.
76. Gibson, "Sixth Ridge," 59.
77. Calhoun in Gibson, "Island in the Past," iv.
78. Ibid., vii.
79. Robert S. Neitzel, letter to Charles Fairbanks, April 6, 1954, copy courtesy of Debbie Woodiel.
80. Kidder, "Plazas," 514–32.

6. Stories from Visionaries and Biolocators

81. Brain, *Tunica Treasure*.
82. Gibson, *Ancient Mounds*, 5.
83. Ford, "Puzzle," 466–72; Haag, "Excavations," 30–31; Ortmann and Kidder, "Building Mound A," 66–88.
84. "Angels or Demons," *Banner-Democrat*.
85. Hauck, *Haunted Places*.
86. Ford, "Additional Notes," 282–85.
87. Joseph, "Poverty Point," 183–89.
88. Ibid., 186.
89. Ibid., 187.
90. Ibid., 187–88.
91. Ibid., 188.
92. Ibid.
93. Ortmann, "Temporal Perspective," table 1.
94. Kidder, "Climate Change," 195–231.
95. Ibid.; Fagan, *Long Summer*.
96. J. Ward, *Ancient Archives*.
97. Walthall, et al., "Galena Analysis," 133–48.
98. Ford, "Additional Notes," 282–85.
99. Apostol, "Effigy Mounds."

Once Upon a Time on the Great Mound

100. Harris, "'Bigfoot,'" 1, 3.
101. Calhoun, "Fox," 3–10.
102. Ford, "Puzzle," 466–72; Willey and Phillips, *Method and Theory*, 159; Kidder, Ortmann and Arco, "Singularity," 9–12.

BIBLIOGRAPHY

Apostol, Andrei. "North American Indian Effigy Mounds: An Enigma at the Frontier of Archaeology and Geology." Paper presented to a meeting of the Society for Scientific Exploration, 1994.

Banner-Democrat. "Angels or Demons—Yap Family Tells What They Saw." September 18, 1997, 6–7.

Brain, Jeffery P. *Tunica Treasure.* Vol. 71. Papers of the Peabody Museum of Archaeology and Ethnology. Cambridge, MA: Harvard University, 1979.

Brookes, Samuel O. "Cultural Complexity in the Middle Archaic in Mississippi." In *Signs of Power: The Rise of Cultural Complexity in the Southeast.* Edited by Jon L. Gibson and Phillip J. Carr. Tuscaloosa: University of Alabama Press, 2004, 97–113.

Bushnell, David I., Jr. *The Choctaw of Bayou Lacomb, St. Tammany Parish, Louisiana.* Washington, D.C.: Bureau of American Ethnology, 1909.

———. "Myths of the Louisiana Choctaw." *American Anthropologist* 12 (1910): 526–35.

Calhoun, John. "Island in the Past." *Louisiana Archaeology,* no. 14 (1991): iii–xiv.

———. "Season of *Bakbak,* the Red-Headed Woodpecker." *Louisiana Archaeology,* no. 12 (1994): ix–x.

———. "The Season of the Fox." *Helicon* 17 (1989): 3–10.

Campbell, Thomas N. "The Choctaw Afterworld." *Journal of American Folklore* 72 (1959): 146–54.

Clark, John E. "Surrounding the Sacred, Geometry and Design of Early Mound Groups as Meaning and Function." In *Signs of Power: The Rise of Cultural Complexity in the Southeast*. Edited by Jon L. Gibson and Philip J. Carr, 162–213. Tuscaloosa: University of Alabama Press, 2004.

Connaway, John M. "The Keenan Bead Cache: Lawrence County, Mississippi." *Louisiana Archaeology* 8 (1981): 57–81.

Connolly, Robert P. "1998 Annual Report: Station Archaeology Program at Poverty Point State Historic Site." On file with Louisiana Division of Archaeology, Baton Rouge.

Crawford, Jessica. "Archaic Effigy Beads: A New Look at Old Beads." Unpublished master's thesis, Department of Anthropology, University of Mississippi, 2004.

Cummings, Linda S. "Box 9.3. Poverty Point Objects." In *Ancient Starch Research*. Edited by Robin Torrence and Huw Barton. Walnut Creek, CA: Left Coast Press, 2006, 182–84.

Cushman, Horatio B. *History of the Choctaw, Chickasaw, and Natchez Indians.* Greenville, TX: Privately printed, 1899.

Doré, Kay Legendre. "Shaman's Crystal." *By the Shining Bayou Waters: The 1995 Excavations at Poverty Point, Louisiana*, no. 13 (1997): xii–xiii.

Ellerbe, Jenny, and Diana M. Greenlee. *Poverty Point: Revealing the Forgotten City.* Baton Rouge: Louisiana State University Press, 2015.

Fagan, Brian. *The Long Summer, How Climate Changed Civilization.* New York: Basic Books, 2004.

Ford, James A. "Additional Notes on the Poverty Point Site in Northeastern Louisiana." *American Antiquity* 19, no. 3 (1954): 282–85.

———. "The Puzzle of Poverty Point." *Natural History* 64, no. 9 (1955): 466–72.

Ford, James A., and Clarence H. Webb. "Poverty Point: A Late Archaic Site in Louisiana." *Anthropological Papers* 46, no. 1 (1956): 5–136.

Gibson, Jon L. *Ancient Mounds of Poverty Point, Place of Rings.* Gainesville: University Press of Florida, 2000.

———. *Archaic Earthworks of the Lower Mississippi Valley, Interpretations from the Field.* Baton Rouge: Louisiana State University Press, 2019.

———. "Broken Circles, Owl Monsters, and Black Earth Midden: Separating Sacred and Secular at Poverty Point." In *Ancient Earthen Enclosures of the Eastern Woodlands*. Edited by Robert C. Mainfort, Jr. and Lynne R. Sullivan, 17–30. Gainesville: University Press of Florida, 1998.

———. "By the Shining Bayou Waters: The 1995 Excavations at Poverty Point, Louisiana." Report no. 13. Center for Archaeological Studies, University of Southwestern Louisiana, Lafayette, 1997.

————. "Cool Dark Woods, Poison Ivy, and Maringoins: The 1993 Excavations at Poverty Point, Louisiana." Report no. 12. Center for Archaeological Studies, University of Southwestern Louisiana, Lafayette, 1994.

————. "Earth Sitting: Architectural Masses at Poverty Point, Northeastern Louisiana." Edited by Kathleen M. Byrd. *Louisiana Archaeology*, no. 13 (1990): 201–37.

————. "In Helona's Shadow: Excavations in the Western Rings at Poverty Point, 1991." Report no. 11. Center for Archaeological Studies, University of Southwestern Louisiana, Lafayette, 1993.

————. "Island in the Past: Archaeological Investigations at the Francis Thompson Site, Madison Parish, Louisiana." *Louisiana Archaeology*, no. 14. (1991).

————. "Mitchell Hillman, 1943–1987: A Tribute." Edited by Kathleen M. Byrd. *Louisiana Archaeology*, no. 13 (1990): 253–67.

————. "Poverty Point State Historic Site, LA." In *American Indian Places, A Historic Guidebook*. Edited by Frances H. Kennedy, 83–84. Boston: Houghton Mifflin, 2008.

————. "Search for the Lost Sixth Ridge: The 1989 Excavations at Poverty Point." Report no. 10. Center for Archaeological Studies, University of Southwestern Louisiana, Lafayette, 1990.

Gill, Sam D. *Native American Religions: An Introduction*. Belmont, CA: Wadsworth, 1982.

Haag, William G. "Excavations at the Poverty Point Site: 1972–1975." Edited by Kathleen M. Byrd. *Louisiana Archaeology*, no. 13 (1990): 1–39.

Hargrave, Michael L., and Berle Clay. "Interim Report: A Magnetic Field Gradient Survey at Poverty Point, January 2006." On file at Poverty Point State Historic Site, Epps, Louisiana.

Harris, Wesley. "Does 'Bigfoot' Haunt Claiborne Woods?" *Guardian-Journal* 37 (Thursday, September 10, 2020): 1, 3.

Hauck, Dennis William. *The National Directory of Haunted Places*. Sacramento, CA: Athanor Press, 1994.

Hunter, Donald G. "The Cicada in Southeastern Archaeology and in Coushatta Tradition." *Louisiana Archaeology*, no. 2 (1975): 219–26.

Jackson, H. Edwin. "Adaptive Systems in the Lower Mississippi Valley During the Poverty Point Period." *North American Archaeologist* 30, no. 3 (1989): 174–204.

Johnson, Jay K. "Poverty Point Period Quartz Crystal Drill Bits, Microliths, and Social Organization in the Yazoo Basin, Mississippi." *Southeastern Archaeology* 12, no. 1 (1993): 59–64.

Joseph, Frank. "Poverty Point." In *Sacred Sites, A Guidebook to Sacred Centers & Mysterious Places in the United States*. Edited by Frank Joseph, 183–89. St. Paul, MN: Llewellyn Publications, 1992.

Kidder, Tristram R. "Climate Change and the Archaic to Woodland Transition (3000–2500 cal. BC) in the Lower Mississippi Valley." *American Antiquity* 71, no. 2 (2006): 195–231.

———. "Plazas as Architecture: An Example from the Raffman Site, Northeast Louisiana." *American Antiquity* 69, no. 3 (2004): 514–32.

Kidder, Tristram R., Anthony L. Ortmann and Lee J. Arco. "Poverty Point and the Archaeology of Singularity." *SAA Archaeological Record* 8, no. 5 (2008): 9–12.

Mayer, Fredrick J. "Appendix D. Ground-Penetrating Radar (GPR), Subsurface Testing, Poverty Point." In *Digging on the Dock of the Bay(ou): The 1988 Excavations at Poverty Point*, 211–18. Report no. 8, 1993.

Moore, Clarence B. "Some Aboriginal Sites in Louisiana and Arkansas." *Journal of the Academy of Natural Sciences of Philadelphia* 16, no. 1 (1913): 7–93.

Mueller, James W., ed. *Sampling in Archaeology*. Tucson: University of Arizona Press, 1979.

Ortmann, Anthony L. "Placing the Poverty Point Mounds in their Temporal Perspective." *American Antiquity* 75, no. 4 (2010): 657–78.

Ortmann, Anthony L., and Tristram R. Kidder. "Building Mound A at Poverty Point, Louisiana, Monumental Public Architecture, Ritual Practice, and Implications for Hunter-Gatherer Complexity." *Geoarchaeology*, no. 28 (2013): 66–88.

Patten, Robert. "Measuring Time and Distance in Ancient Louisiana, 2014." On file with present author, Lake Claiborne, Louisiana.

Paxton, Meredith. *The Cosmos of the Yucatec Maya: Cycles and Steps from the Madrid Codex*. Albuquerque: University of New Mexico Press, 2011.

Renfrew, Colin, and Paul Bahn. *Archaeology, Theories, Methods, and Practice*. 3rd ed. London: Thames & Hudson, 2000.

Shea, Andrea B. "Botanical Remains." In *The Peripheries of Poverty Point*, 245–60. Pollock, LA: New World Research, Inc., 1978.

Stuart, Gene S., and George E. Stuart. *Lost Kingdoms of the Maya*. Washington, D.C.: National Geographic Society, 1993.

Swanton, John R. *Indians of the Southeastern United States*. Washington, D.C.: Bureau of American Ethnology, 1946.

———. *Myths and Tales of the Southeastern Indians*. Washington, D.C.: Bureau of American Ethnology, 1929.

———. *Social Organization and Social Usages of the Indians of the Creek Confederacy.* Washington, D.C.: Bureau of American Ethnology, 1928

———. *Source Material for the Social and Ceremonial Life of the Choctaw Indians.* Washington, D.C.: Bureau of American Ethnology, 1931.

Turner, Johney S. "Strange Things from the Past?" *West Carroll Gazette,* June 25, 1998.

Vaughan, Greg. "The 1988 Poverty Point Field School: Doin' It 10 Centimeters at a Time." In *Digging on the Dock of the Bay(ou), The 1988 Excavations at Poverty Point,* by Jon L. Gibson, xix–xxii, Report no. 8. Center for Archaeological Studies, University of Southwestern Louisiana, Lafayette, 1989.

Walthall, John A., Clarence H. Webb, Stephen Stow and Sharon Goad. "Galena Analysis and Poverty Point Trade." *Midcontinental Journal of Archaeology* 7, no. 1 (1982): 133–48.

Ward, Heather D. "The Paleobotanical Record of the Poverty Point Culture: Implications of Past and Current Research." *Southeastern Archaeology* 17, no. 2 (1998): 166–73.

Ward, John A. *Ancient Archives Among the Cornstalks, Twenty-Seven Century Old Documents on Stone Regarding a Commercial Enterprise of Mediterranean Colonists in the Wabash Valley of MidAmerica.* Vincennes, IN: MRD Associates, 1984.

Webb, Clarence H. "Archaic and Poverty Point Zoomorphic Locust Beads." *American Antiquity* 35 (1971): 105–14.

———. "The Fox-Man Design." *Newsletter of the Louisiana Archaeological Society* 2, no. 3 (1975): 6–7.

———. "The Poverty Point Culture." *Geoscience and Man* 17 (1977).

Willey, Gordon R., and Philip Phillips. *Method and Theory in American Archaeology.* Chicago: University of Chicago Press, 1958.

Wright, Alfred. "Choctaws: Religious Opinions, Traditions, etc." *Mississippi Herald* 24, (1828): 178–83, 214–16.

SUGGESTED READINGS

General

Ellerbe, Jenny, and Diana Greenlee. *Poverty Point: Revealing the Forgotten City*. Baton Rouge: Louisiana State University Press, 2015.

Gibson, Jon. *Ancient Mounds of Poverty Point, Place of Rings*. Gainesville: University Press of Florida, 2000.

Technical

Gibson, Jon. *Archaic Earthworks of the Lower Mississippi Valley, Interpretations from the Field*. Baton Rouge: Louisiana State University Press, 2019.

Webb, Clarence. *The Poverty Point Culture*. 2nd ed. Baton Rouge: School of Geosciences, Louisiana State University, 1982.

ABOUT THE AUTHOR

 **J**on Gibson is an archaeologist and retired professor. He is the author of *Louisiana Piney Woods Oil Boom* (2019) and *Archaic Earthworks of the Lower Mississippi Valley* (2019).

Visit us at
www.historypress.com